Finally
FREE

BREAKTHROUGH FROM PSYCHOLOGICAL AND EMOTIONAL
TRAUMA

Finally
FREE

EDITH BUTLER
FOREWORD BY: R. KEVIN MATTHEWS

Dedication

To God be the glory for the wonderful things He has done. It is indeed an honor to dedicate this book to members of my family who were characterized in this narrative. They are no longer with us but remain forever in our hearts and memories. To my loving mother Clara, beloved sister Mildred, husband Michael, and first cousins Henry and Rodney — you are all missed and were loved dearly and unconditionally. To my lovely daughter, Ecole — you mean everything to me. Thank you for my grandson, Michael, whom I love so very much. Richard Kirby, you've been such a great confidant and friend. Thank you for standing by my side for so many years. I appreciate you. Mary A. Alston, thank you for being my BFF as our relationship has evolved over the years. Though everyone is not listed on this page, I'm thankful to other family members and friends for their support. Lastly, this book is dedicated to all victims suffering from the devastating effects of alcohol addiction and drug abuse. It is my heartfelt prayer that you will seek the help that's needed for recovery.

TABLE OF CONTENTS

PREFACE

The behavior of most individuals addicted to drugs or alcohol will definitely affect the emotional and psychological states of themselves and those who love them. It's just a matter of time before the behavioral change will manifest itself. Most often, the person who compulsively consumes alcohol or drugs rarely stops drinking and drugging successfully. They cannot do it on their own or quit cold turkey. Therefore, they need to seek professional counseling to establish their overall well-being.

After becoming the caregiver for various family members who became chronic alcoholics and drug abusers, I felt it was necessary to share my story with others. Having to witness my family members die from their addictions — repeatedly — took its toll on me. I wrote this book to provide hope for those who suffer from drug addiction and alcohol abuse. It speaks of the devastating effects that substance abuse had on my family members and how I endured seeing them succumb to this disease. If you or someone you love has an addiction to drugs or alcohol, there are organizations and resources available to you. Please, I encourage you to seek help if you, a family member, or friend is unable to break free from substance abuse. Utilize the services that are outlined in this book; treatment facilities are available to help.

Watching a loved one struggle with their dependency may cause you to feel discouraged, but don't give up. Their addiction does not allow them to be sensitive to others. The obsession to ingest drugs and alcohol is great; often causing them to act out of character. Though it may be difficult, the best thing to do is love them throughout their addiction. Remember, substance abuse is a disorder; your loved one is sick. Please don't judge them for their addiction. Talk to them often and let them know you love and care for them unconditionally. Always remember to keep your loved ones close and forgive them for any pain, shame, or embarrassment you experienced. 1 Corinthians 13: 4-7(NIV) states, "Love is patient, love is kind. It does not envy, it does not boast, it is not proud. It does not dishonor others, it is not self-seeking, it is not easily angered, it keeps no record of wrongs. Love does not delight in evil but rejoices with the truth. It always protects, always trusts, always hopes, always perseveres. As a Christian, this Scripture resonates with my spirit as we must always demonstrate love for one another. Be blessed.

FOREWORD

Alcohol and drug abuse can be detrimental to the overall well-being of anyone who gets caught in the throes of addiction. They tear away at a person's health by deteriorating the body, mind, and spirit. If an intervention does not take place for these individuals, the aftermath is not only devastating to them but to their family members (caregivers) who are left to pick up the pieces when death becomes the end-result. People with addictive personalities do not realize going in, how drugs and other substances can destroy their bodies. 1 Corinthians 3:16-17 (NIV) states, "Don't you know that you yourselves are God's temple and that God's Spirit dwells in your midst? If anyone destroys God's temple, God will destroy that person; for God's temple is sacred, and you together are that temple." When we value ourselves by demonstrating self-love, we will take care of our minds, bodies, and spirit by not poisoning ourselves with various substances. Our bodies indeed are our temples and we should be mindful of what we put in our being. Whether it is overeating, extreme drinking, a sexual addiction, or drug use, these addictions can cause many to lose sight of themselves and go into a downward spiral that they are unable to come back from.

In Finally, Free, Edith Butler shares her family's addictions and how caring for them impacted her life incessantly. Being a caregiver is far from an easy responsibility, especially when the caregiver is caring for a parent, spouse, or loved one who ends up dying from a debilitating illness as a result of struggling with substance abuse. This important responsibility of making sure that family members are cared for is a biblical one. 1 Timothy 5:4 (NIV) says that adult children should "Put their religion into practice by caring for their own family and so repaying their parents, for this is pleasing to God." When a caregiver sees to it that their parents are taken care of, they are also obeying the Bible's command to honor their parents; Ephesians 6:2-3 (NIV). The Bible does not contain specific instructions on being a caregiver; however, it provides examples of men and women of faith who did so. Ruth migrated to her mother-in-law's country and worked tirelessly to care for her. Jesus, shortly before he died, designated a caregiver for his mother, Mary (who was apparently then a widow). Finally, Free contains principles that can help caregivers deal with the physically, emotionally, and exhausting challenge of caring for loved ones who wrestle with addiction.

This book takes an in-depth look into the life of Edith Butler, who ended up becoming a caregiver for several family members. As difficult as it was for her to watch each relative slowly sink into deteriorating health, she selflessly gave of herself and placed her needs on the back burner to care for each one. Experiencing levels of stress, anxiety, anger, and frustration, Edith realized that self-care was essential when taking care of others. It is important to know how to manage the emotions that are associated with the stress and grief that come along with dealing with the loss of a loved one. In addition to eating well and getting adequate rest, taking breaks when possible to keep a clear mind is a must. This book offers resources for anyone who is addicted to drugs and alcohol and for the caregivers who are tasked with caring for these individuals. It is enlightening. It is encouraging. It is a must-read.

R. Kevin Matthews
Senior Pastor, The Shepherd's House
International Christian Church

INTRODUCTION

At last — a phenomenal breakthrough from psychological and emotional trauma attributed by overwhelmingly distressful events. This is my truth. My story. My testimony. My life. This is a candid depiction of painful incidents that took place in my life as a result of alcohol and drug abuse by various family members. Remarkably, I persevered and survived the painstaking task of taking care of family members with addictive personalities. God gave me the strength and delivered me from the shackles of shame that kept me bound as a result of their addictions. He set me free — He can set you free as well.

This autobiography was conceived from an unexpected breakthrough while studying the principles of Christian discipleship. It is about my life and how I survived entrapments that stemmed from my childhood through young adulthood. It is an honest account of discovering the addictive personalities of family members who became slaves to substance abuse. For many years, alcohol and drug abuse infiltrated my family. Because of this, my overall well-being was severely impeded. My mother, husband, sister, and cousins were chronic alcoholics — some were drug abusers as well. As a result of their dependencies on various substances, it brought about severe anxiety in my life.

Finally, Free is designed to transform your life from a place of hopelessness to a state of peacefulness. If you are inclined and determined to overcome emotional trauma, take this journey with me and witness the manifestation of a new life of peace and contentment.

There are many circumstances in life that can cause traumatic suffering. Many distressful events can come from self-indulgence or the actions of others. This book speaks to the impact that substance abuse has on the person who's addicted to it and how it affects their families and friends. It is my desire that Finally, Free will give hope and encouragement to substance abusers and the ones they love. If you are a victim of physical, emotional or psychological trauma, I encourage you to seek individual or group counseling. There are many professional organizations and resources available to you and your family. Finally, Free also provides insight into the biblical truths of God's love for us during challenging times in our lives.

One thing that is constant in life is change. Our lives can change in an instant. One minute we may be up and the next, we are down. As we journey through life, a tragic event can change the landscape of our lives; thus, causing us to turn to a stimulant as a coping mechanism. Be it drugs, alcohol or another form of addiction, we all have our vices. The death of a loved one, the loss of a job, some form of abuse (sexual, emotional, psychological, or physical), or an illness are traumatic events that can be viewed as triggers that can launch a person into an addiction. None of us are exempt; this can happen to anyone of us. What do we do in the event that it happens to us, a friend, or a family member? Do we look down on the individual with an addictive personality? Do we offer assistance? Or do we love them in their addictive states?

Ephesians 4:32 (KJV) states, "Be kind and compassionate to one another, forgiving each other, just as in Christ God forgave you." As Christians, we are to always demonstrate love, compassion, and forgiveness toward one another. No matter what we go through in life, it's good to know that someone cares; someone loves us and is available to us despite the troubles we may encounter. Loving someone who is addicted to drugs or alcohol can be challenging; nevertheless, we are to love them. We must help them through this tumultuous time. Addictions, left untreated, can and will lead to death. As Nancy Reagan, wife of former President Ronald Reagan, said in her anti-drug campaign back in the 1980's, Just Say No to drugs and other forms of substances. It's just not worth it in the end.

CHAPTER 1

Clara

1924-1982
I Love You Mama Forever

It is extremely important to have a mother, mother figure, or guardian who can offer wise counsel when we have to make life-changing decisions. They can share their own childhood experiences and serve as a role model. This guidance is essential and significantly important for a female child. Most mothers play a vital role in the development of their daughters' self-esteem and overall welfare. Unfortunately, I did not have the typical relationship between a mother and daughter. The majority of my social interaction and childhood developmental experiences were from my grandmother Amanda, the matriarch of our family and my Aunt Beadie. Sadly, my mother's consumption of alcoholic beverages was her priority. She simply did not have the ability to devote to a healthy relationship with me due to chronic alcoholism. This addiction robbed me of the mother–daughter bond that I so desperately wanted with my mother. We all have our shortcomings, and this was hers. Despite that, she was my mother and I loved her, nonetheless.

My mother was a stunningly full-figured woman, with smooth cocoa brown skin and dark brown round eyes. She had a beautiful smile and wore it gracefully. She stood about 5'8 inches tall without high heels. She had jet black hair that was often styled in a short cut

and tapered close to her neck. My mother was an impeccably dressed woman and coordinated her entire wardrobe with all the necessary accessories. She sported fancy hats, beautiful dresses, skirts, laced gloves and sheer stockings like nobody's business. Her dresses and suits accentuated her full figure and gorgeously shaped legs. Everything she wore was in its proper place. The colors she chose to wear were matched with charming jewelry, leather handbags, and colorful scarves. She was most assuredly what some would call a fashionista in today's society.

My mother was very personable and could capture the attention of those in her presence with her alluring wide smile. When she walked into a room it was definitely a display of confidence and poise. She was not shy and was always willing to pose for the camera. I am definitely my mother's daughter; I also love taking pictures and posing for the camera. Additionally, she loved hand dancing, singing, and listening to rhythm and blues, and jazz. Charles Brown was her favorite blues singer. He was a pianist who performed during the 1940s and 1950s. Merry Christmas Baby was one of his hits that became a legendary success. This was one of her favorite songs and she would sing it all the time. My mother and her friends would go uptown to The Howard Theater in Washington, DC, a predominately African American theatre, for a night out on the town. This historic theater opened its doors in 1910. Since it was located near Howard University, this led to its name. The Howard Theater was where the socialites got dressed up and enjoyed world-renowned artists. During the 1950's and 1960's, it became an entertainment venue for rock 'n' roll and rhythm and blues. Some of the legendary artists who graced the stage were: Sarah Vaughan, Billie Holiday, Duke Ellington, Louis Armstrong, Ella Fitzgerald, Lena Horne, Cab Calloway and James Brown, just to name a few. During their heyday, my mother and her friends dressed up to the nines and were always ready to hit the town for an evening of dancing, laughter and fun.

While my mother enjoyed having a good time with her friends, there was another side to her that was always disturbing and perplexing to me. I was about 10 years old when I started noticing my mother's constant alcohol consumption. Her drinking intensified over the years and became severe to the point that it affected her physical and mental health. It was obvious my mother had slowed down and was more tired than usual. She was not her happy-go-lucky self. Honestly, I believe she had given up on herself and life in general. She seemed exhausted about her entire situation. My mother consumed alcohol the majority of her life. She was incoherent when under the influence of alcohol. I could not deal with her state of mind and I hated seeing her in that way. My grandmother was also disappointed with her daughter. Her expectations for all of her children were to excel and distinguish themselves in every respect. In view of the fact that my mother's drinking intensified and became excessive, it really affected my grandmother's disposition. She was dissatisfied with her daughter and the path she chose to go down. Becoming an alcoholic was not what she envisioned for her child. The chronic drinking was something we could not process. It became an obsession that she could not shake. Nevertheless, we loved her immensely. We knew this was a struggle for her.

At a young age, I wanted better for my mother. I simply could not understand why she could not see what I saw in her — that she was capable of doing more with her life. I wanted her to have a better life for herself. From my perspective, she was complicated. I could not comprehend why she would continuously drink. My friends' mothers were stable and ideal models that I longed for in my life. When I was about 13 years old, I went on a weekend trip with my friend's family. While on vacation, I stepped on a piece of heavy equipment I could not see in the vast field of weeds. Consequently, my ankle was swollen, and I could not walk on it. When I returned home, I was hopping on one foot. My friend's mother was a nurse and she attended to my injury. Since we lived a few doors from each other, she took me home to explain to my mother and grandmother about the injury. My mother was drunk at a time when I really needed her, and it was embarrassing. Upon realizing my mother's intoxication and her being incoherent, the neighbor spoke directly to my grandmother instead. The shame of my mother's drunken state was visible on all of our faces.

My mother consumed alcohol every day and the only exception was when she was hospitalized for alcohol poisoning or detoxification. After a few weeks of detox and the sickness subsided, the cycle would resume; more alcohol consumption, more hospitalizations. These events lasted for nearly 20 years. My mother was not boisterous when she drank. She was soft-spoken and mild-mannered and did not like conflict and aggressive arguments. When she was intoxicated, she would listen to music and was otherwise relatively quiet. She also liked to dance at times when she was under the influence of alcohol. Unlike other alcoholics in my immediate family, who would argue and fight, my mother was the extreme opposite. Their behavior was so intolerable, even she would not want to be around them. My mother simply enjoyed drinking, listening to music and dancing, which fulfilled her self-esteem. She seemed happy and at peace when she danced.

When I look back in time, there were many photos of my mother and her friends having a good time. The number of alcoholic beverages that were available for consumption was visible in the backgrounds of the photos. In some, she appeared to be in her early twenties. I suspect it was her social drinking that eventually developed into chronic alcoholism. Most of the time, I was appalled at her and her friends' drinking and made it a point to stay away from them as much as possible. This was not a difficult decision because my mother moved away from our household when I was about 10 years old. She lived with her boyfriend who was a really nice guy. I loved him like a biological father. He was awesome in how he treated me and my friends. He spoiled me and taught me how to drive. He would take my friends and I to the movies, skating rink, and other places where teenagers often hung out. Of course, he drank as well; however, he was never a drunk but drank enough to feel good. In today's terms, he was "nice." My mother's boyfriend was overall, a really nice guy and I'm glad he was there for me. I'm grateful that he loved and cared for my mother in the state she was in.

Since I lived with my grandmother Amanda, grandfather John, Aunt Beadie and my sister Mildred, I visited my mother during the week and on weekends. Most of my visits were brief because I simply did not like some of her alcoholic friends. On the first and the third of the month, it was a routine for my mother and her close friends to purchase alcohol. They would cash their retirement or social security checks and "get the party started." Typically, I would not make contact with my mother because I was well aware of all the drinking that would take place. It was my preference to stay away from all the drama. Often, they were loud, and I did not like seeing their obscene behavior. Their topics of discussion were of no interest to me as a child because I had no place in grown folk's business anyway. When they were drunk, they were not too concerned about what was going on in my little world. Instead they were busy talking about someone else who had gotten drunk, whose money was stolen, or fights that had taken place. For the times that I visited my mother for dinner, and she was not inebriated, we laughed and talked about my life and how I was doing. I liked when we spent times like those together and I wanted to keep things that way. On those rare occasions, it was important to me not to share any difficulties I may have been experiencing. I did not want my mother to worry about any of my issues. As far as she was concerned, my life was good.

It's interesting that I do not recall being asked whether I wanted to live with my mother or grandmother. If I had been given a choice, I would have preferred to live with my grandmother because I needed stability. I'm glad that I ended up staying with her for that very reason — every child needs to be in a stable environment. Even at the tender age of 10, I realized the importance of stability. The fact that I was no longer living with my mother was not an issue for me. My feelings toward her never changed and I knew I would see her on certain days. Regardless of my mother's chronic alcoholism, I loved her as any child would love their parent. She and I were able to spend special moments together. When she was not intoxicated, she would talk with me and tell jokes. I loved her sense of humor. If I was sad, she always found a way to put a smile on my face. We would often recite her favorite poem which made us both feel great, titled "In The Morning," written by Paul Lawrence Dunbar. He was an African American poet, novelist and playwright of the late 19th century and early 20th century and a graduate of Howard University.

Even though she was dysfunctional, she was my mother and her gentle personality made it easy to love her even more. My mother loved me and was proud of me despite it all. This I was certain of. She often told me how I never gave her any trouble. Because of my character I believe it minimized some of her problems. My mother was proud of my school and community activities. During my school years, my focus was primarily on studying. I became active in black history studies in high school. At the age of 14, I was a hospital volunteer candy striper a

the District of Columbia's General Hospital for Sick Children. Candy stripers work under the direct supervision of nurses. As a volunteer, I read stories to the children and assisted them with eating and getting dressed. The children of our neighborhood club made arts and crafts to give to the children. I have always been affectionate towards children, especially those with disabilities. Because I was so active, she was not worried about any major problems where I was concerned. I was her good girl. This might have provided her with some peace and that was somewhat comforting to me.

Even though my mother and I no longer lived together, it was reassuring to know that she was still nearby. She lived in an apartment not far from where I lived. Sad to say, after long-term drinking, my mother was incapable of paying her monthly expenses. Her sister, my Aunt Beadie, received my mother's checks and paid all of her expenses for over 15 years. I just hated how alcohol changed her into a different person; one who was rendered irresponsible. As I matured and examined her life more carefully, I suspected there was turmoil in her spirit because her demeanor was normally quiet. Judging from her facial expressions, she seemed tormented; definitely not at peace. There was a certain level of discontent. I suspected that whatever she had to deal with, it was too much. She would rather be in a state of intoxication rather than face reality. Regrettably, I did not ask the questions that would have answered some of my concerns. I'm not sure if the reason why I failed to ask questions was because in my young mind, I might have thought that harmful circumstances would have been conjured up that would have contributed to a steady decline in her health.

On March 4, 1982, my mother became very sick and was rushed to the District of Columbia General Hospital. It was my nephew, Chauncey, who called me at home to inform me that my mother had passed. The entire family was shocked when we received the telephone call to come to the hospital to make an identification of her body. Aunt Beadie was too distraught to do it. Therefore, as the most stable member of my immediate family, I identified my mother's body at the morgue. I was 28 years old when this terrible event occurred.

The loss of a parent or loved one at any age is difficult to accept and the adjustment is just as hard. As a young adult, I never entertained the idea of my mother passing away while I was young. I expected her to live to a ripe old age. Even so, under the circumstances of her health, I was keenly aware it would be sooner rather than later. When I saw her body, I was in shock; I could not deny what was right before me. It was so hard to process. I felt so sad that everything had abruptly ended. Our conversations and spending any more time together were now over. I felt so alone, as if I was in this world all by myself. Questions circled around in my head: Who do I turn to now? Who will understand how I feel? What do I do now? I certainly could not look to my Aunt Beadie because she was having a difficult time dealing with the death of her sister as well. They were very close. This was one of the saddest days of my life. I felt so numb with tears constantly pouring out my eyes and streaming down my face. I sobbed and sobbed. I was puffy-eyed and lachrymose; I was crushed. I felt some guilt because I had not seen her for at least a week. There was no closure to tell her how much I loved her; to give her a hug and to look into her face one last time.

My mother's death had me in a dark place. There was no light illuminating anywhere. Despair had settled in my spirit. Depression invited itself into my life. I cried for days, months, and years even. I felt somewhat responsible even though I could not help my mother. Maybe if I would have gone over to her apartment and stayed with her, she would have hung in there a little longer and not leave me? Maybe if I would have talked to her more about quitting for my sake, just maybe she would have tried harder to quit the habit. I kept wondering what I could have done differently to change the outcome. I felt I could fix everything, but the fact of the matter was that I simply could not. I had to realize that I could not control the actions of grown adults. As much as I wanted to help my mother, it was out of my hands. I wanted a stable relationship with her and tried to control things which were out of my control.

Upon seeing my mother's dead body, I felt as though I'd lost a part of myself. Certainly, I was aware that at some point this would happen. But you can never prepare for such a dreadful event. Without a doubt, I always wanted to take care of my mother and make her happy. I felt she deserved to be happy. Now that she was no longer with me, there was a tremendous void. It was in this moment that I looked to God to help me deal with the varying emotions that were running through me. I needed Him to help me through this mourning process. There is no pain like it. Feelings of hurt, sorrow, despair, anger, regret and even blame can easily saturate the mind. To counteract these emotions, I had to get on my knees and pray to God. I needed Him to help me deal with the wave of emotions that surfaced daily. I cried out to Him and asked Him to heal my broken heart. All I knew to do was pray, pray and pray some more. To keep my eyes focused on Him, I listened to Christian music that often lifted my spirits. Each person mourns differently. This method worked for me and I encourage others to seek God during times like this. The emotions that are felt fluctuate with each passing day. One minute it appears that all is well, then the next thing you know, the floodgates open up and you cannot contain the tears. My advice is to embrace the emotions as they come. If you feel like crying, cry; if you feel sad, feel the sadness; if you feel the need to laugh at a good memory, laugh. Don't be afraid to release the emotions that you feel; it is alright to do this. Believe it or not, this is part of the healing process. Another thing to consider is getting counseling or seeking medical assistance to aid in this natural progression or phase in our lives. Unfortunately, we will all have to face it at some point in our lives. It is important to seek the help we need. Sometimes the pain is too hard to bear, and it's necessary to get medical and/or psychological assistance.

In summary, if you are blessed to have a good mother with whom you can engage in "girl talk" and share your innermost personal secrets, consider yourself fortunate. Don't take the relationship for granted because there are so many individuals who would love to trade places with you. There are rarely second chances or do-overs in life so we should show how much we love our loved ones before they leave this world. As the saying goes, "Give them their roses while they are alive." Cherish them while you can. If you are estranged from your parents, I strongly encourage you to make an effort to reconcile any differences. Though we are adults, we are never too old to want the affection, time, and undivided attention of a devoted mother's (or father's) love.

Experiencing the absence of a responsible mother can develop into feelings of despair and a sense of loneliness. There is hope as there are responsible women who can serve as a substitute for the unhealthy relationship that you've had with your mother. You can find reassurance in another woman or male figure. Sometimes our biological parents are not able to care for us as they should but know that there are individuals out there who can provide you with the love and support you need. If you have a parent who is addicted to substances, I encourage you to be there for that parent. Talk and ask questions. It can prove to be beneficial to you and that individual as well. You don't want to find yourself in a situation that I was in where I had the opportunity to engage in meaningful conversations and failed to act upon them. Learn from my mistakes. Had I had a conversation with my mother, I'm convinced it would have brought about closure to some issues I was ignoring. Do not hesitate to talk with your parents, guardians or loved ones. I implore you to ask questions. You may get relief from your emotional pain. Unfortunately, I neglected to ask my mother questions. I wish I'd asked questions regarding her relationship with my father. If I had a second chance, some of the questions I would have asked her are: How did you meet my father? Did you love my father? Did you encounter abuse in previous relationships? Were you ever molested? What were your goals and dreams? Do you have any regrets? These questions would have been good to ask because it would've given me a better understanding of my mother. It would have provided a greater understanding into why she felt the need to drink her life away. Perhaps abuse transpired in her life and she didn't want to share it with anyone. Nonetheless, it is important to have the dialogue as it could make significant progress in healing from emotional trauma. Sometimes we may feel like we have time; like our parents are always going to be around. I wish I would have taken advantage of our time together. There were many instances of wanting to know more about my mother's life. If you have not experienced the loss of a mother, I encourage you to reach out to her regardless of her being on drugs or alcohol. You'll never know, showing continuous love towards her and showing her that you will never give up on her can be what's needed to push her in the direction of healing.

My mother Clara died of cirrhosis of the liver at the age of 58.

25

Michael

1952-1984
I Love You Forever In
My Heart

Michael was my late husband and the father of my only child, Ecole. He was a decent man and it was apparent that he came from a loving family; good stock. He was articulate, thoughtful of others and had astute mannerisms. He had a lot of charm, popularity, and was a smooth talker. Michael could brighten anyone's day with his wit. He and I met and graduated from Eastern High School in Washington, DC. Michael was very popular in high school and in his senior year was nominated "Best Dressed" of the year. We became close friends and eventually our relationship evolved into a loving relationship. We shared similar interests in books, the arts, and music. Some of our activities included going to church, movies, jazz festivals, parties, vacations, and so much more. Michael graduated a year prior to me and one year after I graduated, we were married. Prior to our marriage, in the Fall following his graduation, Michael was accepted to attend Knoxville College as the recipient of the Martin Luther King, Jr. Fellowship Scholarship. He proved that college was not for everyone. After one year of college, he returned home to Washington, DC and secured employment with the District of Columbia Government, Office of Contracting and Purchasing. Michael was a Purchasing Agent and continued employment in this capacity for almost fifteen years until his untimely death.

Our initial plans were to marry in Rock Creek Park in Washington, DC at a charming and secluded area. Unfortunately, it rained and consequently the ceremony was moved indoors. I was almost 20 years old when we exchanged our wedding vows. It took place at St. Timothy's Episcopal Church in Washington, DC on April 28, 1973. Our wedding ceremony was modest and intimate. Attendees included my parents, cousin Ann and a few friends. Michael's mother, sister, aunts and first cousins were in attendance. My parents did not attend my wedding reception, however. My mother and cousin Ann were preoccupied with buying alcoholic beverages to fix their alcohol addictions. According to Ann, they could not wait until the ceremony was over to go to the liquor store. The craving was so strong that she compared the compulsion to drink to salivating for food. My father left after the ceremony, perhaps he had another agenda. The only family member who attended my reception was my Aunt Beadie. My sister Mildred lived out of state and cousins Henry and Rodney were too ornery to attend. Even though some family were not able to attend the wedding or reception, a memorable highlight of the ceremony was when we both took a sip of bitter and sweet wine. Our officiate and close friend imparted a symbolic gesture of wine to represent what to expect in marriage as well as in life. He explained that we would experience some good days (sweet wine) as well as challenging and difficult days (bitter wine). This was a different outlook on marriage, but very realistic. Marriage is about taking the good with the bad. This was something I learned in my own marriage.

Michael and I subsequently joined St. Timothy's Episcopal Church and we were a very happy and young couple. After three exciting years of marriage, I gave birth to a baby girl on December 10, 1976, whom we named, Ecole. One of my cousins suggested her first name and Michael gave the middle name, Natosha. It is without question; Ecole was everything to us as parents. We adored her and devoted our time to foster her confidence and self-esteem. It was our intention to ensure she had everything she needed to have a happy and successful life. I enjoyed motherhood because Ecole was and still is such a gifted and lovable daughter. Since my relationship with my mother was unstable, I committed to becoming an excellent mother to my daughter. It was important to devote the time towards her development and invest in her overall well-being. Because we had only one child, our focus was primarily on her welfare. After her birth, I was fortunate that I was able to stay home and care for her for almost a year. I cherished that period in our lives because it allowed me to bond with my child. Having this time with her cemented our relationship from that point until present day.

Being Ecole's mother brought pure joy to my life. I was fortunate in that I did not experience any negative experiences such as postpartum depression as some women tend to do after birthing a child. My motherly instincts kicked in once she was born. It was important to me to make sure I cultivated a strong mother-daughter relationship with her. I was determined to ensure that she received from me what I lacked from my mother — attention and affection. I made sure I was present and active in her life. As new parents, Michael and I maintained our focus on her development. We invested in private school education and extra curriculum activities. Some people might have characterized Ecole as being spoiled because of how we doted on our baby girl. She was a blessing to us and was our only child so, yes — we did spoil her. We were happy and caring parents who wanted the very best for our daughter. We participated in her activities and school field trips. She was active in tap dance, in church ministry and we made sure she attended Sunday school. It was important to us that she had a spiritual upbringing. Ecole brought so much joy in our lives. Michael absolutely adored his daughter. You could see it in his eyes. There were times when I would catch him staring at her as if to say, "Look at what we have made?" Ecole was our pride and joy. She was the glue that kept us going. She was our world.

Sadly, I was an immature teenager when I married my husband. At 19, I did not see the flashing signs, the red flags that waved: caution, beware, stop, look, and listen. I said to myself, "It's not that bad. It's not a big deal." I turned a blind eye to all the warning signs because I was desperately focused on escaping my dysfunctional family. I witnessed Michael's drinking and drug use and thought to myself, "He drinks a lot and occasionally uses drugs. Who is this man that I've married?" Why I didn't confront what I saw then was beyond me. The truth is, I didn't realize or want to accept the fact that he might have a serious problem. In my mind, his drinking was only being done in social settings; in fact, that was how it started. But the social drinking manifested into almost daily drinking. Obviously, in the beginning stages, I could not foresee that it would not get any better, only worsen over time. I was in denial and wanted to believe that he would stop using substances. Part of the denial was based on the fact that he was a functional alcoholic and drug user. He went to work every day and functioned like a "normal" person. Michael never crossed the line that his actions could subsequently land him in prison or cause him to get an arrest record. I don't recall him ever getting a minor traffic ticket. Because of the positive behavior he exemplified, I had some hope that things would get better. It was so obvious that he was different from most substance abusers. On occasion, he would stand on the street corners dressed to the nines in professional dress shoes and clothes. He was absolutely an impeccable dresser from head to toe as he took great pride in his appearance. Michael would starch his shirts and iron them and it was apparent they were "tight"; almost flawless. He simply did not resemble someone who was a drug user. He disguised it well. Some of the men and women who stood with him on the street corners were degenerates. Many had declined in all manner of humanity. They often looked disheveled in their appearance. He wasn't by himself; he did have a few functional friends who consumed alcohol and drugs as well. These particular friends were professional men who were married, had children and matriculated from college. One of his closest friends who participated in alcohol and substance abuse was a former college basketball player. It goes to show that you cannot judge anyone based on outer appearances.

Honestly, I thought I had some influence, an intellectual perspective, to change his destructive behavior. During this particular time, I was accustomed to helping dysfunctional family members and here I was again trying to rescue another individual. Certainly, I did not like being in this situation again. Michael consumed drugs and alcohol from the inception of our marriage, and it escalated into his latter years. It started to become too much to handle. The absolute turning point for me was the onset of his seizures. I knew at this point in the marriage I could take no more. Without a doubt, I knew it would not be long before he died. I could no longer witness the decline in his mental and physical health. According to Dr. Andrey Stojic, of Epilepsy Center, Fairview Hospital, in Cleveland, OH, he states that excessive alcohol can impact the excitability of brain nerve cells. This in turn can spur abnormal electrical brain activity that causes seizures. Michael's seizures lasted about a month and I was certainly aware that his time on earth was nearing the end. I could see death in his eyes. They appeared glassy and it seemed he looked past me; through me. The drugs and alcohol took over his body. They had a hold over my husband and there was nothing I could do to change his situation.

By entering into this lifetime commitment, I realized marriage was an opportunity for me to get away from my own family dramas. This was the wrong approach to take into my marriage. I did not have sufficient knowledge about marriage and what was involved in maintaining a good and healthy one. Because I was so young, I was not at all concerned about this partnership or its longevity. Dealing with a young child, family matters, and keeping up with my job consumed my world. It took a toll on me after a while. I was like an injured bird that needed some tender loving care. What I did not realize was that Michael was incapable of providing the care that I needed. I was deceived into thinking that marriage would be the change that I needed to deal with the hurt and pain that I felt in dealing with my family. What I did not realize was that Michael had his own dysfunctions and demons to deal with. How could he help me when he needed help himself?

What was unfortunate was the fact that I unknowingly married a man who was broken and needed healing as well. I did not realize how much he was seriously hurting because he was mourning the loss of his brother, Reginald, who was murdered in 1972. It was a shock among family and friends when Reginald died because he was a quiet and soft- spoken guy. He didn't seem like the one to get into any trouble or who had enemies, so his murder was surprising to everyone. Michael and his brother were about two years apart. Though they argued frequently, it was very apparent how much they loved each other. They socialized together as young adults and even lived together for a while. Still dealing with the loss of his brother, Michael then had to cope with the loss of his parents, Reginald and Catherine.

The death of a loved one is hard to deal with but it's even more difficult when it's your immediate family — parents and siblings. It was about this time that our marriage shifted. Michael grieved for many years and I believe the culmination of those events led to him turning to the drugs and alcohol even more to cope with the pain he was under. This, no doubt, led to his eventual demise. He could not rebound from the losses. Accepting and processing the grief he was under brought on stress in our household. Sorry to say, I did not examine his behavior and his eventual recreational drinking and drug use. His moods would change sporadically where he seemed happy in one instance and then sad, depressed, and withdrawn at other times. His unstable behavior affected my moods because I did not know what to expect from him at any given moment. Sometimes he would be excited to see Ecole and I, but we did not always know what to expect from him with each passing day.

It was several years into our marriage that Michael began to consume more alcohol and drugs, especially on the weekends. There were times when he would drink and use drugs the entire weekend. Being a functional alcoholic and drug user, he managed to maintain a career and hid his addiction from some people. His constant drug use was in clear view and caused me to shut down completely from him. Ecole and I would spend our time having social outings at the park, zoo, or museums to escape his debilitating episodes or tantrums. On the few occasions when he was not getting "high" we went to church, the movies, and took vacations like a normal family. Other times, I would be so disappointed when I looked at him because I knew it was going to be a dreadful weekend. One of the things that bothered me the most about his drug use was when he nodded off. I would call Michael's name countless amount of times and he was unresponsive. Time and time again, this particular behavior caused my heart to beat frantically. The truth is, I was not sure if he was experiencing a medical crisis or not. My emotions wavered based on his erratic behavior. It was like being on an emotional rollercoaster. If Michael was not "high" I was elated. If he was under the influence, my mood changed to frustration and anxiety.

After many years of this emotional vacillation, it became extremely difficult to deal with his behavior. His drug use escalated from the weekends into some weekdays. Distraught that my husband was in this condition, I often spoke with him about getting help. Continuously, he refused treatment; I was at my wits end. Seeing Michael losing himself to alcoholic seizures was hurtful to me. I so desperately wanted to help my husband as I hated seeing him in this way. It broke my heart that even though I offered to go with him to treatment, he always refused. The first seizure I witnessed was when we were sitting at the dining room table having a general conversation. All of a sudden, Michael's head collapsed on top of the table. When he finally raised his head off the table, I could see his eyes moving rapidly and he was looking upward towards the ceiling. I called out his name several times and he did not respond. When he did not respond to my voice, I was aware that he was unconscious for a few seconds. After the seizure, he and I continued talking as if nothing had happened. Unlike most, his seizures did not cause him to experience convulsions or twitching. He simply would lose consciousness for a few seconds. At this particular time, there was no point in talking about getting help. He had already passed the point of no return, but I remained compassionate. It was really unfortunate to witness knowing there was no relief in sight for him and that he had done this to himself. At this stage, he was nearing the end of his life. I could only reassure him that we loved him very much. He seemed grateful that I tried to help him but could not in the end. He often remarked about how I was a "good woman" who stood by his side during turbulent times. It seemed to me that Michael was ready to leave this earth. It seemed he was tired of it all — he felt defeated.

Michael went through all of the stages of alcoholism. In the early stages, a couple of symptoms include an intense pleasure with drinking and a preoccupation with alcohol. In the next phase, symptoms include withdrawal, blackouts, personality disintegration and denial. In the final stage, there is irreversible physical and mental deteriorations. The cravings for alcohol are so overpowering that an addicted person becomes a slave to the substance, having no control over the impulse to take another drink. I felt he was at the final stage of it when his behavior became reckless and he became very argumentative. Michael was no longer himself and had already passed the point of no return. The quantity of his purchase of alcohol had increased and his behavior became typical of a deteriorating alcoholic. According to Katherine Ketcham, William F. Asbury, Mel Schulstad and Arthur P. Ciaramicoli, Ed.D., Ph.D. states: "At this stage the disease seems to have progressed into irreversible physical and mental deterioration. In the final stages of alcoholism, the drive to drink is so ferociously demanding that alcoholics often feel they have no choice but to obey the addicted brain's commands. Getting alcohol to the cells is the first priority, over time, it becomes the only priority."

The last few times I saw him before his death, there were changes in his appetite and he was no longer interested in food. Michael was restless and agitated because of the pain he was in. He was starting to look emaciated. There was no doubt in my mind that he was going to die soon; death was knocking at his door. There was no way he could continue in the direction he was going in. In spite of the decline, he somehow remained gainfully employed. The fact that he still worked to support his family under the circumstances was commendable. However, I feared that if he did not get into a detox program immediately, he could die at any time. In his final days, he was like a "ticking time bomb." I didn't know when and/or where he would explode. I knew for a fact that the explosion was imminent, and it was going to be hard to pick up the pieces. As I watched my husband's condition worsen, one of my greatest fears was that I would find him laying somewhere in the streets. If something like that would have happened, the embarrassment of that event would have forced me to relocate to another city. It was my duty to protect my daughter. The shame of something like that happening would have been too much to take on. It was in my best interest and the well-being of our daughter to separate. By this time, it was my belief that Michael had lost all hope.

According to Harmony Recovery Group, nodding off on heroin is extremely dangerous and may be indicative of a much more severe condition, such as a life threatening overdose. Heroin is a potent sedative that can make it challenging or impossible to remain awake upon administration.

Since I had experienced some turmoil with my mother's addiction, it was too much to endure with my husband's deteriorating condition. Being in the presence of alcoholics and drug users, I had grown accustomed to the range of emotions associated with those with addictive personalities. Major outbreaks such as fights, arguments, and other outrageous behaviors always surfaced because the drugs and alcohol had taken a hold of them. I witnessed this type of dysfunction for too many years. I could not continue to endure the instability of my husband and remain normal. For the sake of my daughter, I pushed through the drama and confusion that my husband offered us. I had no choice; otherwise, I'm certain I would've had a mental breakdown. The welfare of my daughter was what mattered most. It was in my best interest, as a mother and wife, to separate from him because he was simply too far gone. He moved out of our home and secured an apartment. After he refused treatment so many times, I could not witness the state of his despondency any longer. I didn't want our daughter to observe him in this manner either. Nearing the end of his life, his consumption of alcohol increased to the point where I felt that maybe he just gave up and wanted to die. I wanted to save him, but I could not. I felt so sad for our daughter, but thankfully she was too young to witness and retain what was going on with her father. Our daughter was seven years old when Michael died. It wasn't until she was a teenager that I shared this aspect of his life with her.

Even though Michael had his flaws, he loved his daughter. And she loved him back. In having conversations with Ecole about her father, I know that if he were alive today, she would express how much she still loves him. Ecole was very fond of her father. She shared with me some of her most memorable experiences of her father. She loved how good he always smelled and remembers how he always kept lots of colognes stored in his bathroom. Another great memory of hers was when she was about seven years old and spent the night at her dad's apartment. The next morning, they woke up and made breakfast. Michael provided her with a step stool so she could cook bacon and scrambled eggs. One evening they were watching television and a program came on about making a donation to a charitable organization. He asked her if she wanted to donate to this worthy cause and she agreed. Michael made contact with the organization and made the monetary donation. Ecole was elated that she participated in this worthy endeavor. One of her most memorable recollection of her dad was when she was in the first grade. On Ecole's seventh birthday, he surprised her at school with a dozen yellow roses. She remembered that she was blushing and felt so special. As her father, Michael always made her feel not only special, but safe and protected. Notably, he always made her feel important — that she mattered.

In conclusion, perhaps Michael was troubled about many

things in his life, some of which I was not privy to. But I remained supportive of my husband through some of the darkest periods of his life. In spite of that, what do I know for sure? Despite his alcohol abuse and drug addiction, he loved me, his daughter, and his extended family immensely. He absolutely ensured we lacked nothing. He was a responsible father who provided for his family even with his addictions.

Alcohol and drug abuse result in declining and out of control behavior. Substance abuse affects and alters the mind. I didn't pay attention to my husband's drug tendencies; therefore, I went from one bad situation to another. Apparently, there was trouble in Michael's soul that he was unable to talk about. In reality, he and I were two wounded souls, each having our own personal issues that should have been healed well before we merged into a marriage.

Michael died of cirrhosis of the liver at the age of 31.

CHAPTER 3

Rodney

1961-1996
I Will Love You Forevermore

Rodney was my first cousin. His mother, my Aunt Beadie and my mother were sisters. Rodney and his brother, Henry, were seventeen years apart in age. In view of that fact, it caused contempt on the part of Henry as the oldest brother. He was not receptive to having a younger brother. Because of the significant age difference between the two, it was difficult for them to develop a wholesome and loving relationship. The fact that they had the same mother and different fathers might have also influenced their broken relationship in some way. It's safe to say, they were not close by any stretch of the imagination. It is my opinion that Henry was jealous of his brother and when under the influence of alcohol, he sometimes expressed his resentment and displeasure. I surmised that since he was no longer the primary focus of his mother's affections that he never bonded with his younger brother. Rodney and Henry's relationship was estranged. They definitely did not behave like loving brothers. Most often, their interchanges were subtle and sometimes distant.

Rodney did not talk much at all and never expressed his deepest feelings, at least not to me. He had such respect and high regard for me, and our interactions were always pleasant. He was exceptionally quiet and reserved. When we had family gatherings, we never knew he was in the room at times because he was so quiet. He primarily kept to himself and did not bother anyone. Even though he had a quiet disposition, something he and I had in common, he was not ambitious. He had no interest in learning and studying. As a result, Rodney did not complete his high school education because of his misjudgments. He lost his focus at about 13 years old. He lost interest in school and eventually dropped out. He had no interest in the typical activities of a teenaged boy, such as sports or video games; however, he did have an interest in girls. Though he was reserved, he did have an affinity for a particular young lady. The family was surprised of her devotion to him because she was responsible and did not use drugs. She really loved him and was smitten by him. It was evident that his charming and quiet personality attracted women to him in spite of his addictions. They dated for several years after high school until he became too sick.

Prior to that, Rodney associated with older teenagers who appeared like they were destined to end up in a life of crime. Once he got involved in hanging on street corners and using drugs, this became his normal behavior and routine. He lived to get high and associated with undesirable characters. During this time, I was married and was not totally aware of everything that was going on with him. I had some knowledge but was not aware of the day-to-day events. Rodney had potential. When he was in his twenties, he sang with a group of guys. Even though I never heard him sing with the group, I was told he could really sing. Be that as it may, he did not pursue this gift and ended up temporarily securing employment in custodial services. Sadly, the majority of his life was spent in the streets abusing alcohol, heroin, and other drugs. Heroin was his drug of choice; it was his candy.

In the late 1980's, the District of Columbia government received a federal government grant to provide treatment, reduce opioid addiction, and reduce fatal overdoses. This grant allowed Rodney to participate in the methadone program for his heroin addiction. Sometimes, Aunt Beadie and I would take him to the outpatient clinic to get his methadone, a long-acting opioid. One problem with the use of methadone is its potential for abuse; that is, those who are addicted may use their methadone in nonprescribed ways just as they used heroin.

Patients on methadone would line up each morning in front of the clinic window, where a nurse would dispense the daily dose of methadone adjusted for each patient. For many patients, the dosage was not sedating but enough to keep cravings and withdrawal at bay. 8 Individuals with drug use disorders deserve nothing less than ethical and science-based standards of care that are available similar to the standards used in treatment of other chronic diseases. ©UNODC/ World Health Organization International Standards for the Treatment of Drug Use Disorders, 2016.

While the methadone was supposed to help Rodney with his cravings, there were times when it did not help him. Maybe he ran out or just didn't take the appropriate dosage. On a particular Christmas holiday, my cousin Ann discovered Rodney in the bathroom near death from a heroin overdose. It was disturbing to see him in this condition. Ann and I were overcome with shock and disbelief. Aunt Beadie and other family members were laughing, talking, and having a good time, oblivious to what we stumbled across. Ann had gone upstairs to use the bathroom and found Rodney laying on the floor with a needle in his arm. She called downstairs for me to come up to the bathroom. We didn't want to tell his mother because witnessing this would've hurt her to the core. We saw the sadness that was in her eyes because her son was addicted to drugs. She often tried to talk to him in hopes that he would turn his life around, but it fell on deaf ears. She became complicit in the situation. She could have put him out of her home, giving him "tough love" but the idea of her son being homeless caused her to think otherwise. It's been said that women have a soft spot for their sons. I guess this explained why she tolerated his behavior. As an assistant pastor, in addition to talking with him, she constantly prayed that he would change his ways, but it seemed pointless — he needed professional help to defeat his demons.

Embarrassed by what was playing out before us, we tried to figure out the best course of action to take. We did not want to inform his mother, especially in the presence of other family members and friends. We had no other choice but to tell her. Ann and I called Aunt

Beadie upstairs to the bathroom and she immediately knew what was going on. Seeing her son overdosed and laying on the floor, she was paralyzed with shock, unable to do anything. Ann and I handled it. That was my first time witnessing something like that; it may have been hers too. Once the ambulance arrived, Rodney was revived and the EMT informed us that there was no need to take him to the hospital and that he would be fine. I'm not sure what they gave him to drink but he was better after that. The other family members were oblivious of what had transpired in the upstairs bathroom. We played it off as if Rodney had a severe ache of some kind. Ann, Aunt Beadie, and I listened to the technician's assessment and Rodney got himself together and eventually left the house. We were not forthright in telling other family members about what happened. The actual truth was not revealed. How much shame and embarrassment can one family endure? Rodney's addiction to heroin was so strong that even though he had the overdose scare on Christmas Day, he continued using it and living the street life. He could not shake it, and this would ultimately lead to his death.

In the early 1990's, and several years later, Rodney was charged with a misdemeanor crime for possession with intent to distribute narcotic drugs in Washington, DC. He was incarcerated at Lorton Correctional Facility in Lorton for this charge and served several months. Years later he returned to prison for the same charge where he served less than a year. Since he was incarcerated for a brief period, there was no substance abuse rehabilitation centers around for him to join. After his release from prison, Rodney resumed his normal activities of standing on street corners — buying, selling, and using drugs.

In 1995, Rodney's mother died suddenly in the home we grew up in. Going to the prison to inform him that his mother died was one of the most difficult visits I had to make. I contacted the prison chaplain and explained to him the circumstances. I was adamant that I wanted to tell him about his mother. I did not want any official to deliver the sad news. My request was granted, and my cousin Ann and I went to the corrections facility to meet with Rodney. I remember vividly. Our visit was during the work week. When the correctional officer escorted him to meet us his eyes were large like saucers. The look on his face asked, "What are you doing here?" My stomach was in knots. The closer he walked towards us the sadder and sicker I became. We did not sit down. I looked him directly into his sad eyes and told him I had some bad news. I said, "Rodney, Beadie passed." I did not give him any details, nor did he ask for any. He was in shock. Ann and I hugged him and told him how much we loved him. In classic Rodney style, he was quiet and had nothing to say. His reaction was not shocking to us because that was his demeanor. He turned and walked back to his cell to process the news he had just received. It was such a heartrending moment as we watched him walk away.

I became Rodney's power of attorney after his mother died and ended up planning her funeral as well. Her homegoing service was held at the Baptist church where she was an assistant pastor. Honestly, in my opinion, I believe the stress of having two dysfunctional adult sons who were hooked on drugs and alcohol was extremely overwhelming and taxing on my aunt. I believe it eventually caused her death. During this particular time, my adrenaline was at its highest point. I had absolutely no appetite. I was only focused on making sure I executed the funeral arrangements in such a way that Rodney would be able to attend his mother's wake. I felt I had to make it happen without fail for Rodney's sake. I hated that he was literally alone, unable to be with his family at the time. The majority of this burden was on my shoulder to handle. Being classified as "the strong one" implied that I would get things done precisely. What choice did I have? I had to get it done. As Rodney's power of attorney, I had to make numerous telephone calls to the correctional facility and funeral home. The clergy from my aunt's church and I prepared the homegoing service. I arranged with the prison facility to request Rodney's release to attend his mother's wake. It was imperative to provide an exact time of the wake to accommodate the transport of Rodney to the funeral home. He was granted release since the charge he faced was only a misdemeanor. He was escorted in shackles by prison officials to the funeral home where he was able to say his goodbyes to his mother in private. The family was not permitted to be at the funeral home during his visit. I could only imagine the tremendous anguish he felt when he saw his mother laying in a casket and then having to return back to a prison cell to grieve alone. Though everything seemed to have gone smoothly during the process, it was disheartening to witness Rodney seeing his mother alone without the benefit of his immediate family. I could only imagine how he felt.

After the burial of Aunt Beadie, I worked tirelessly to get Rodney out of prison. Upon being medically released, he lived with his brother for a few months. After a few days at home, I planned the largest welcome home party with a few family members and close friends. We had an array of food and fun. Rodney was elated to be home. Unfortunately, shortly after his release from prison, he became extremely sick from all the drugs he had used prior to and after his return home. He was taken to the District of Columbia General Hospital and decided after a few days that he was not going to stay there. I received a telephone call from the attending physician that Rodney was leaving against medical advice. He had to know the end was near. A year after his mother's death, like his mother, Rodney died in the home we grew up in.

With his mother's death, I was certainly aware of the inevitable; Rodney would not live a long life due to his reckless lifestyle. So, his death came as no surprise. As I mentioned previously, Rodney was quiet and did not cause trouble inside the home. But it was brought to my attention from a family member, that Rodney was ruthless in the streets. I was told he was not to be challenged in any way because he was a brutal fighter. He could lay someone out and hurt them terribly; sometimes causing them to end up in the hospital. From what I understood he had a reputation and was not to be messed with. Thankfully, I never witnessed this side of him. It was not until after his death that I learned all these dreadful things about him. Although I learned these apparent truths, it never stopped me from loving him unconditionally.

After all the deaths in my immediate family, I became numb of all normal feelings. I began to question God: How much more do I have to endure? When will I get some normalcy back in my life? I was craving some inner peace. I was tired of the stress my body was under. I lost my appetite, felt nausea, had muscle tension, headaches and had difficulty sleeping. The stress was so intense. I felt like I was going to have a heart attack at times. I took deep breaths and had to go on short walks to clear my head. Honestly, when I reflect on those circumstances, I know it had to be God giving me the strength to keep moving. In retrospect, I did not realize God was with me all the time. If I did not have God in my life, I believe I would have died from the overpowering sorrow that I felt. I was a perfect candidate for therapeutic help. After so much death and seeing my family diminishing around me, I welcomed the idea of being able to lay on a couch to talk things out. I needed something like that for my sanity. My maternal family's composition was moderate. I was not a part of a large family and it seemed everyone around me was dying. It was imperative that I sought professional grief counseling for depression after Rodney's death. His death affected me for many years. The impact from his death was phenomenal to me because I truly could not understand why I was so shattered by it. Many years later, I surmised my unrelenting misery was triggered by his mother's death the previous year. Another aspect to my grief was based on the fact that prior to Rodney's death, I worked tirelessly to get him medically released from prison. I knew that at some point he would pass away and watching him deteriorate almost daily was emotionally draining. His troubles in life were based on his own doing. But I felt a tremendous sense of empathy and stress at the same time as I inadvertently took on his burdens. I don't recall him ever mourning the loss of his mother. Like me, he kept so much to himself.

In losing a loved one, we don't always know how to respond. We cannot always control our emotions. We may suppress our emotions for a while, but ultimately, the pain must be released. And rightfully so. Grief comes with a wave of emotions. One minute it seems like we are fine and the next, the floodgates open up and our eyes are full of tears. We deal with the emotions as they come but it's important to experience and release the varying emotions each time they show up. Never bury them. The healthy thing to do is cry, laugh and talk through the emotions. Though we did not take the same path in life, I loved my cousin. I was honored to be his primary caregiver as I was able to be with him in his final days. I know this meant a lot to him. It did for me as well.

Rodney died of cirrhosis of the liver and other complications at the age 34.

Henry

1944-1999
I Will Always Love You

Henry was my first cousin, my mother's sister's oldest child. He was the oldest grandchild for at least six years before my sister Mildred was born. Of course, being the first grandchild, he received all the attention and affection from our grandparents. By the time I was born, he was already nine years older than me, so we weren't very close in our early years. After graduating from high school, he married and decided to go into the Army to support his wife. He served a few years and apparently wanted to come home. I don't know what he told the Army officials, but he was honorably discharged. I guess he missed his wife. Sadly, his marriage of only a few years, ultimately ended in divorce. He never remarried and did not have any children. He returned home to live with his mother, our grandparents, brother Rodney, my sister Mildred, and myself.

Henry attended college but did not graduate and ended up working in several clerical positions with the District of Columbia government. After a while, he began to associate with some of his high school friends. They would often go out together to parties, which of course included drinking alcohol. After many years of drinking and partying, he ultimately became an excessive drinker which led to him becoming an alcoholic. I wasn't sure if he used any drugs. During the

time I spent with him, I only saw him consume alcohol. From getting his fill of alcoholic beverages, what I did observe was that he was an angry and violent person when he drank too much. He was verbally abusive, argumentative, and got into physical altercations. There were times when he was nice and fun to be around. There were other times when he would turn on a dime and we would wonder, "Who is this man?" It was like he had a sudden personality change. After a while, this became his expected behavior — he was always inappropriate and was known for disturbing the peace in our home.

As I grew older and eventually moved out of the house, I did not engage with him often. He lived on his own for several years, and without any notice or request, one day he moved back into the family home. This was a turning point for the family household, which now consisted of my grandparents and his mother. He moved in and ruled the house! There was some fear the family experienced when he was intoxicated. Because of his inappropriate and unpredictable behavior, he made occurrences and family get-togethers very uncomfortable. I remember a time when Henry and some of his friends were at our home drinking, talking, and listening to loud music. Most of the time, the music was always too loud. All of a sudden, he abruptly told his friends to "Get out!" Those were his favorite words. Family and friends would remark and laugh hysterically about how he would put people out of the house. His friends tried to convince him that everything was ok, but he was insistent that they all leave. Eventually they did leave. After they left, we would hear Henry talking out loud to himself and crying that he had no friends.

My nephew Chauncey shared with me an incident he vividly recalled about Henry. As usual, Henry was playing his music entirely too loud. His mother had asked him numerous times to turn it down. He ignored her and kept playing it anyway. At the time, Chauncey was about 15 years old and decided enough was enough. He grabbed his baseball bat and smashed Henry's entire stereo system. Needless to say, things were quiet for a while and in his anger, Henry stopped speaking to Chauncey for some time. He knew not to try and attack or question Chauncey because it would not have ended well for him. Chauncey was a fighter as well and would have literally knocked him out. Henry made no demands and had to "suck it up" and eventually he purchased another stereo system. There was another occasion where he was intoxicated and was about to jump out of a third-floor bedroom window. He had only one leg partially dangling out of the window. Mildred was present at the time and told him to just go ahead and jump. Apparently, he did not have the courage to do so and decided to pull himself back into the house. After creating a ruckus, everything was settled and back to "normal" as if nothing had ever happened. Henry's intoxication caused him to do some irrational things. There was yet another encounter where he was absolutely belligerent and pulled a long kitchen knife on my grandfather. I don't know what prompted him to do it. I recall his mother pleading for him to stop. Eventually, he came to his senses and put the knife down and went to his room. I had just arrived at the house and it was another day of Henry's drama.

Henry was totally obnoxious, and we were aware that he was either drunk or hung over. Otherwise, when he was not drinking, he was quiet as a church mouse. According to Drug Use & Abuse, every drinker probably has had at least one somewhat delayed consequence of an episode of overindulgence — the hangover. Hangovers begin to appear about 4 to 12 hours after reaching the peak of blood alcohol concentration (BAC) and generally are not considered a pleasant alcohol effect. Symptoms may include headaches, dizziness, nausea, vomiting, increased heart rate, fatigue and thirst. A consistent finding in many studies of beliefs about the effects of alcohol is that it increases power and aggression (Goldman, Darkes, & Del Boca, 1999).

After Henry had the latest outburst in front of the entire family, where he pulled the knife out on my grandfather, we all knew he needed help. Chauncey later informed me that an argument ensued because my grandfather no longer wanted Henry to live with them. He apparently had had enough of his charades. It seemed that his behavior was a cry for help, and we recognized that to be the case. Henry made several attempts to become sober, but they all failed. He attended Alcoholics Anonymous meetings and other support groups, but these didn't yield any positive results. Perhaps if he had sought help earlier, he may have had a different outcome.

According to Alcoholics Anonymous local treatment centers often have trained interventionist on staff or can put you in touch with one in your area. You may want to contact the Association of Intervention Specialists (AIS) for a list of members in your area, at www.associationofinterventionspecialists.org. AIS members guide families and friends, business executives, and others through the intervention process whereby a person addicted to alcohol and/or other drugs and compulsive behaviors is encouraged to accept help.

During his latter years, he was unstable and could not maintain employment. Henry became homeless for a while and ended up getting sick. He was admitted to Washington DC Veteran's Medical Center. Subsequently, he was transferred to Joseph's House. This hospice facility provided healing care to homeless men and women with late-stage and end-stage AIDS and terminal cancer through physical nurturing, spiritual companionship, and the restoration of dignity. Inevitably, I ended up having to take care of him. Somehow this responsibility managed to fall into my lap once again. As Henry's caregiver, I took excellent care of him during his stay at hospice by providing him with healthy snacks and beverages, ensuring all his medical needs were addressed and taken care of expeditiously. I talked with the medical staff to determine if he needed additional medication or alternative prescriptions to minimize some of his pain. There were a few times he was taken to the emergency room for shortness of breath while he was in hospice. On better days when he was feeling up to par, we planned activities that he enjoyed. This seemed to cheer him up at times. On other occasions, he would visit me at my home and stay the entire day, especially on Sundays. I played gospel music the entire time he visited so that the messages from the songs would seep into his spirit. He often slept nearly eight hours because of the heavy doses of medication he was on. During this time, he had almost no appetite and drank non-alcoholic beverages because he was too sick to consume alcohol. When it was time for him to depart, he would tell me he had a good time, although he slept most of the time away. I'm convinced that his soul and spirit needed to rest in that environment. There's nothing like being in a familiar and comfortable setting that cause you to be at peace. I knew this made him feel good. As time went on, he and I visited one of his closest friends where we relaxed and talked about life. It seemed like this was about spending quality time with those who were close to him.

As I sensed that time was running out for him, I arranged for pastors and other counselors (outside of the hospice facility) to visit with him, read Scriptures, and to pray with him. When I visited with him, I brought family photos to reminisce about the good ol' days. I thought this was a good idea so he could take his mind off his condition. I also brought some of his favorite magazines such as Ebony, Jet, and Men's Magazine for him to read. I brought him a radio so he could listen to his favorite music stations — Howard University's WHUR and WOL stations. Some of his favorite artists were Gladys Knight, Ray Charles and other rhythm and blues singers. During one of my visits, Henry told me, "Never forget I always loved you." It was his expression to thank me for all the love, care, and compassion I offered him over the years. He was coming to terms with the idea that he was nearing his death and I could only image what he was feeling or the internal turmoil he was experiencing knowing he had done this to himself. Keeping him as comfortable as possible was my primary concern. When he began to deteriorate and could no longer communicate, I made sure I remained in contact with the medical staff and made sure they adjusted the room temperature, played soft music, and checked his vital signs often. Also, I had to be kept abreast of his changing condition as I was responsible for his funeral arrangements. It was heart-wrenching to see him in this way; weak and lifeless. Alcoholism stole my cousin's life. Henry became its victim and it never lost its grip on him.

During my last few visits with Henry, his eyes were opened wide and fixed to the ceiling. All communication had ceased. This was a sure sign he was transitioning from this world. According to a pamphlet on death and dying, it stated that each person's dying process is unique to him or her. I had visited with him earlier in the evening to talk with him for the last time and let him know that I loved him. Shortly after my visit, I received a telephone call that he had passed. I returned to the facility that night to talk with the director. She telephoned the morgue to arrange for the retrieval of his body. The following day, I met with officials at the morgue to arrange for his cremation. That same day, I talked with the hospice director to plan a memorial service which was commonly held at the facility. The director welcomed the opportunity to serve my family. She was a delightful woman and it was apparent she was close to all the residents.

I could not bear the thought of taking his remains from the morgue to hospice for the memorial service. Fortunately, my friend Kirby agreed to handle this aspect of his death. It was a morbid and uneasy feeling to realize as we traveled from one destination to the next that Henry was right with us in an urn. It was a common practice of the director to take some of the remains of the residents and sprinkle them around the facility. I am grateful this particular hospice facility was a pleasant environment and that he was well-cared for during his stay.

Henry died of cirrhosis of the liver and other complications at the age of 55.

Delayed Grief

ealing with the death of a loved one is never easy. During these moments of grief, I did the only thing I knew to do and that was to draw closer to God. Once again, He literally was my source of comfort and strength while caring for my cousin and other family members. I had to cry out to God at times for Him to heal my broken heart and to help me get through the grief. Some people will offer advice, ask too many unimportant questions, and their actions do not help while you are in mourning. They all mean well; they just don't always know the right words to say. And that's okay. Grief can be an agonizing foe and if it is not dealt with can land you into a dark place. Many years after my family members' deaths, I visited a holistic physician. I could no longer carry the pain around anymore and sought help once and for all. The initial question the doctor asked me was how would I have felt if my mother had died when I was 10 years old? The doctor posed this question based on a questionnaire I had completed and upon her review, it prompted her to ask that question. As I recall the questions asked about family relationships, deaths, and other family dynamics, I began to weep. I never liked to cry in front of people, but this time I couldn't hold back the tears. When I actually thought about it, I would have been in great distress if my mother had passed away at that young age. I shocked myself when the tears started pouring out of me. I had suppressed my emotions for so long that the doctor related my physical situation, my tearful reaction, to long-term suppressed grief. The doctor advised me to discuss in detail each loss and how it had impacted my overall well-being. Did the grief prevent me from working? Did I turn away from family and friends? Did I discontinue activities that once gave me pleasure? The doctor wanted me to talk about each loss and how it impacted my relationships. She advised me that I needed to seek counseling in order to move forward in a positive direction and to restore healing. Eventually, I participated in group counseling that was offered at a former church in which I was a member. The counseling sessions were beneficial, and I was on a long journey to recovery.

Delayed grief is common for many who've lost loved ones. What is delayed grief? by Beyond the Influence, Understanding and Defeating Alcoholism, Katherine Ketcham and William F. Asbury explains what this ailment is. It is just that: grief that you don't fully experience until quite a while after your loss. Those who feel a delayed grief reaction often describe it as a devastating sadness that hits them out of the blue. It might arrive a few weeks or months after the funeral or sometimes even years later. So, why does this happen? Sometimes, the shock of a loss or a need to work through immediate practical problems leads us to, consciously or not, "hold off" our grief, it then catches up with us later, sometimes triggered by another loss, or even something small and otherwise inconsequential. Once it arrives, this delayed grief reaction is, in a way, to be welcomed. After all, it grants us the opportunity to work through our feelings and, in time heal.

Once the delayed grief finally hits you, it often feels almost exactly like immediate grief it's just that it might appear to come out of nowhere. Sadness, anger, guilt, raw hurt: it can be a storm of emotions. For a while you might find yourself crying a lot. You might also feel "foggy" or unable to eat, sleep, or cope with your everyday routine. All of these feelings are natural reactions to loss. When you experience delayed grief it is important to: look after your health, talk to your family and friends, make time to think, avoid unhealthy coping strategies (drinking alcohol might numb the pain for a while, but you'll feel a lot worse in the long run) and look for local bereavement support.

In an article written by M. Katherine Shear, MD "Grief and mourning gone awry: pathway and course of complicated grief," she writes: Bereavement refers to the experience of having lost someone close. Grief is the psychobiological response to bereavement whose hallmark is a blend of yearning and sadness, along with thoughts, memories, and images of the deceased person. Insofar as we never stop feeling sad that loved ones are gone, or stop missing them, grief is permanent. Mourning is the array of psychological processes that are set in motion by bereavement in order to moderate and integrate grief by coming to terms with the loss and reorienting to a world without our loved ones in it. Depression is a mental disorder. Grief is not. Bereaved people are sad because they miss a person they loved, a person who added light and color and warmth to their world. They feel the light has been turned off and they aren't sure how to turn it on again. Mourning is the process by which bereaved people seek and find ways to turn the light on in the world again.

According to the National Institutes of Health (NIH), grief can cause physical sensations like tightness and heaviness in the chest or throat, nausea or stomach upset, dizziness, headache and much more. The behavior associated with grief is difficulty sleeping, loss of interest in daily activities, and becoming more aggressive or irritable. The psychological symptoms are guilt, anger, hostility, restlessness, inability to concentrate, and much more. During my grief, I experienced the aforementioned sensations indicated by NIH. As I had to get counseling for my grief, I encourage everyone to do the same. It is not a good idea to hold the grief in. There's help out there; do not be afraid, embarrassed, or think you can tackle this emotion by yourself.

Please reach out to organizations such as:

Hospice Foundation of America (HFA)
1707 L Street, NW
Washington, DC
(202) 457-5811

HFA provides leadership in the development and application of hospice and its philosophy of care with the goal of enhancing the U.S. health care system and the role of hospice within it.

National Hospice Foundation (NHF)
1731 King Street
Alexandria, Virginia 22314
(703) 516-4928

NHF the fundraising affiliate of the National Hospice and Palliative Care Organization is dedicated to supporting the development of resources for individuals and their families facing serious and life-limiting illnesses, raising awareness and increasing access to hospice and palliative care, and providing ongoing professional education and skills development to hospice and palliative care professionals.

****

Amedisys Hospice of Greater Chesapeake
(in Prince Georges County)
1400 Mercantile Lane, Suite 228
Largo, MD 20774
(301) 322-6023

Amedisys provides high-quality hospice care in home health, transport service, nursing services and therapy services.

CHAPTER 6

Mildred

1950-2018
I Love You Today,
Tomorrow & Always

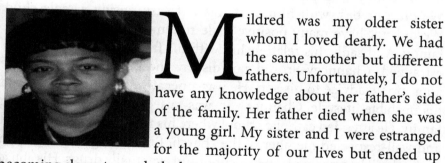

Mildred was my older sister whom I loved dearly. We had the same mother but different fathers. Unfortunately, I do not have any knowledge about her father's side of the family. Her father died when she was a young girl. My sister and I were estranged for the majority of our lives but ended up becoming closer towards the latter years of her life. Mildred possessed a domineering personality and most often wanted her way. If she did not get her way, there was family chaos. She argued with anyone who got in her way, and if necessary, engaged in physical altercations. She and I were opposites in many aspects. I enjoyed school and social activities and she was the troublemaker in school and in the neighborhood. She caused a lot of drama in our family by inciting arguments and initiating fights, especially when she was under the influence of alcohol. I, on the other hand, was quiet and easygoing. Because of this, she antagonized me at times.

From the age of 10, Mildred was labelled the "wild child." There was an incident when she was in the fifth grade where she smacked her teacher in the face. I don't know the circumstances that prompted Mildred to strike her teacher, but my father ended up going to the school to resolve the matter. During her teen years, she grew to be rebellious and was determined to do whatever she wanted; no one could stop her. My mother Clara, Aunt Beadie, and grandmother Amanda, all tried to contain her, but it was a waste of time. By the age of 16, she gave birth to her only child, Chauncey. Because she was so young, Aunt Beadie, my grandmother Amanda and my mother Clara were instrumental in his upbringing. They were concerned for his overall development. I was 13 years old when he was born. What I noticed was that Mildred was doing her own thing and it did not include parenting. She would hang out with friends and sometimes stayed away from home where the family was unaware of her whereabouts. At about 17 years old, I took on the role of being Chauncey's guardian because he stayed close to my side. During this time, he was my only nephew and I had ample time and attention to dote on him. He had several women in our family who provided him with support and encouragement. We did our best with him as it was not easy raising a male child. We did not have many positive male role models in my immediate family. And sadly, his relationship with his father, Chauncey Sr., was estranged. Chauncey Sr. did not display the best behavior or give appropriate advice to his son. He was a negative influence because of his unstable lifestyle. Chauncey Sr. was raised in a stable and loving family. He attended catholic school where his mother was a prominent and well-respected member of the church. Before he graduated from high school he was involved in alcohol and eventually drugs. His abuse became out of control after years of addiction to alcohol. There was an occasion where he consumed significant amounts of drugs and consequently had a stroke. As a result, he could no longer talk or walk and was placed in a nursing home for several months until his death. He died in his fifties. Before his addictions got out of control, he owned a home improvement business named Chauncey & Son. I really liked Chauncey Sr., because he had a keen sense of humor and he respected me. This made it easy for me to love him. I have fond memories of him. What I remember the most was that he always dressed impeccably and was known for wearing penny loafers. It was disheartening that he died a victim of drugs and alcohol abuse. Rather than focus on his addictions, I choose to remember the times when he was gainfully employed and self-sufficient. I'm not sure why Chauncey Sr. and my sister's relationship did not work out but the great thing that came out of their relationship was Chauncey Jr.

Even though my sister had a child out of wedlock and seemed to have had a hard exterior, she still had a soft spot for me as her younger sister. She gave me the nickname "baby girl" and always made it a point to tease me by mentioning that she was three years older than me. She made it clear that she was the big sister. And it was important to her that I looked up to her as such. Interestingly, she didn't particularly want me to be around her friends. Perhaps she was shielding me from a life of destruction. I must say, she was my protector. I recall a particular incident at a night club where a woman had mistaken me for someone else. This woman was angry and wanted to fight me. I certainly did not know her nor was I aware of the circumstance behind her anger. Mildred being who she was, was not one to back down from a fight. Seeing what transpired with the woman and I, she kept her eyes on her and when she went to the bathroom, followed behind her and confronted her. Suddenly, an argument arose and the woman, who was visibly intimidated by my sister, backed down. Thankfully, the incident ended peacefully. Clearly, Mildred was the fighter between the two of us. I tried to avoid conflicts as much as possible. Even though she was my defender, we hardly ever did anything together because we had different lifestyles and different friends. When we were younger, I did not desire to engage in the things that she did because we didn't have much in common. When we did interact, most times it involved getting together for holiday events with the entire family.

Mildred was a feisty and attractive woman. She stood about 5 feet 9 inches tall without heels and was a stunningly slim-figured woman. She wore her hair in many styles, most often curly and cropped on her neck. She was light skinned with beautiful dark brown eyes. I admired how Mildred was not shy at all; if there was a party you would know she was present. She was the life of the party; loud sometimes, laughing out loudly, dancing, and having a good time. Aretha Franklin was her favorite rhythm and blues artist. Sometimes she would play one of Aretha's CD's or albums and sing her heart out and other times she would start crying. Apparently, she could relate to some of the lyrics and this made her feel down at times. On the upside, she knew all the latest dance moves and was fast on her feet. Mildred also loved to dress and was always looking good. It was important for her to be with the in-crowd sporting the latest of everything — designer clothes and shoes, handbags, and jewelry. These things were most important to her self-esteem.

Mildred also had some great attributes. She always maintained an impeccable home; she made sure everything was spotless. If you were drinking a beverage and sat the glass down on the table and eventually reached to retrieve it, she would have the glass already in the kitchen sink and washing it. If someone was smoking a cigarette, she would pick up the ashtray, clean it, and sit it back on the table. She was always cleaning and sometimes she would be told to sit down and relax. Mildred had a lot of nervous energy that made her this way. In addition to her nervous energy, she would sometimes be agitated which was contributed by her alcohol consumption and withdrawals. Another great attribute that she possessed was that she was a great cook. When she was not drinking or getting high, she knew how to throw down in the kitchen. This was one of the traits that was passed on because all the women in my family knew how to cook. It was something we all took pleasure in doing. Ecole, Chauncey, Mildred's boyfriends and other family members enjoyed her cooking. Her favorite and best dishes were fried chicken, cabbage and potato salad. We would finish off scrumptious meals with a tall glass of iced tea. She made some good iced tea too.

Being as attractive as she was, she did not have any issues with attracting men. She had her share of admirers and boyfriends who treated her well despite her addictions. On the contrary, there were others who were physically abusive to her. They also indulged in alcohol and drugs. For the boyfriends who were good to her, it appeared they loved and cared about her and made attempts to prevent her from drinking and drugging. Unfortunately, she was unable to stop drinking and taking prescription drugs. She suffered severely from alcohol consumption, other forms of drugs, and prescription drugs as well. The prescription drug of her choice was Oxycodone (See Appendix A). According to the Drug Enforcement Administration (DEA), oxycodone is like heroin; it creates a euphoric, sedative effect. 58.8 million prescriptions for oxycodone were dispensed in the United States in 2013. Today, this drug is one of the most common that proves to be addictive to anyone who uses it. This drug enticed my sister and kept her coming back for more. Even though I loved Mildred and desired a better relationship with her, it was not possible because of her addictions.

Several years after her son's birth, Mildred moved to Atlanta and lived there for a while. I don't know who she was living with at that particular time. When I got married, she was living in Atlanta and did not attend my wedding. After a few years of living in Atlanta, she decided to relocate to Wilson, North Carolina with her boyfriend, named Knight. She, Chauncey, and Knight worked at Firestone Tire Company for a short while. After a few years, Knight passed away. I don't know whether he was sick or whether he died of natural causes. After his death, Mildred and Chauncey relocated to Raleigh, North Carolina and lived there for many years. Chauncey eventually returned home to the District of Columbia.

My sister might have been a lot of things but one thing she definitely was — was a hustler. While living in North Carolina, she held several jobs as a nurse's aide and also in housekeeping. They were not long-term, however. Maybe the longest she ever worked on a specific job was a year. She was unable to remain on these jobs for extended periods due to being drawn to the street life. There were times when our family was unaware of her whereabouts. She took off often, getting involved in parties and other things that happened in the streets. Unfortunately, the drugs she took caused her to lie, cheat, and steal. She developed cunning ways where she manipulated and conned us out of things such as clothes and money. She did this while she lived in the DC Metropolitan area (DMV) and while in North Carolina. She had to find ways to replenish and satisfy her drug appetite. This behavior is typical of people who have lost their way as a result of drug use. Even though she was entangled with these drugs, I believe my sister protected me from the lifestyle in which she lived. There were many street activities I was unaware of. I assume she shielded me from her life because she was ashamed of who she had become. She did not want me to witness her unsavory behavior. This may have been her intent but when you are addicted to drugs, the unpleasant behaviors will present themselves.

Finally Free

While living in Raleigh and working her different jobs, overtime her excessive drinking caused her to develop problems with long-term standing. This caused great pain in her knees and joints. After many years of living in North Carolina her health began to fail. She applied and was granted disability for diabetes, high blood pressure, and treatment for other chronic diseases. This was the beginning of her decline. Her chronic drinking began to take its toll. Although she was experiencing medical problems, she always paid her rent and other expenses on time. She was self-sufficient for a while but eventually she required a home health aide to assist her with household chores, groceries, and essential shopping. The home health aide worked with Mildred for a short period, because she proved to be irresponsible. On several occasions, she would stop at the liquor store to purchased beer and liquor for Mildred. We had to terminate her services and felt a replacement would not be necessary because Mildred knew how to manipulate people. Once she actually told Chauncey, Ecole and I to "watch this." We watched her manipulate her primary care doctor to write prescriptions for her when it was obvious, she was already overly medicated. She walked directly into the doctor's office, without an appointment, spoke to the receptionist, walked by her desk, and went directly into the doctor's private office. Shortly thereafter, she emerged with a prescription for a controlled substance. She was proud as a peacock. She knew how to manipulate people to get what she wanted. This was something that she mastered over the years.

It was somewhere in her forties and fifties when Mildred developed diabetes that impaired both of her legs. It became difficult for her to walk because her legs and feet were always swollen. She developed skin discoloration and complained of burning and tingling sensations. She ended up having to need a walker to get around because her legs were severely damaged. Eventually, her mobility declined, and she remained in a lot of diabetic pain. Overtime, Mildred was in and out of hospitals for many years. She needed treatment primarily for diabetes and alcoholism. To add to her troubles, her vision was impaired due to an injury she incurred as a result of being in an abusive relationship. At that particular time, she was beating on her boyfriend and got the best of him. He retaliated by striking her in the eye. Because of this severe injury, she lost her eye and was given a prosthetic one where regular treatment was required to maintain it.

60

Mildred endured many hospitalizations and detoxification treatments as an inpatient and an outpatient resident. The family was not allowed to visit or talk to her for several weeks while she was undergoing treatment. The only contact the family had was with the medical staff that kept us abreast of her condition. When she was finally transported back to North Carolina to the hospital, it was disturbing to see her in a mental state of confusion. The side effects of some of the medications caused her to have constant mood swings and she slept too long and soundly. Her diabetes became more difficult to treat and she constantly complained about overall body pain.

Mood swings are a common symptom of many types of addiction, such as alcohol use disorder, opiate dependence and dissociative drug use. Some of the symptoms are anxiety, depression and personality changes. According to the National Institute on Drug Abuse, this is the result of the ways chemicals impact the brain. Seeing Mildred in this condition prompted me to take action. Although I lived out of state, I knew I had to take care of my sister. Around the year 2000, I became more involved in her life and began to take on more of my sister's daily responsibilities. Chauncey and Ecole chimed in to help as well. Ecole was her primary caregiver because they both resided in neighboring cities. I was her secondary caregiver. Often, I visited her in North Carolina when she was sick or was admitted to hospitals for her various health issues. She was admitted for several days or weeks at a time to detoxify from alcohol and drugs. After her stay at treatment centers, I recall countless times being at home and receiving phone calls from out of town that she was being discharged. I always gathered myself to make the four-hour trip to arrange for her discharge. Because her health problems were overwhelming, it became apparent she could not live alone. Arrangements needed to be made for assisted living.

Being in an assisted living facility seemed to be the best alternative to living alone in her apartment. However, it turned out that while this seemed to be the best option for her, it was not. I recall examining all of her medications and determined she was being prescribed too many. The number of prescriptions and over-the-counter drugs were entirely too much. She was taking medicines for heartburn, pain in her legs, insomnia, and chronic obstructive pulmonary disease (COPD), to name a few. COPD is a group of lung disease that block airflow and make it difficult to breathe. She also wore a nicotine patch to cut down on smoking cigarettes. During this time, her primary doctor treated her for these issues. Mildred also received treatment from several other doctors for diabetic foot pain, eye problems and other health issues. Unfortunately, it became apparent to us that her primary doctor took advantage of her condition and addictions. He was responsible for prescribing her narcotic drugs. I didn't quite trust him. I met with him and requested that he discontinued prescribing her narcotic drugs. The primary doctor's response was that she was an adult and entitled to making her own decisions. His response was absolutely irresponsible. It appeared that Mildred often visited his office, without an appointment, and demanded that he provided her with prescriptions for drugs. He had no issues with filling out a prescription slip for her to get the drugs she desired. Ecole, Chauncey, and I were appalled at what we witnessed. We had to get her out of there and away from him. To us, he was an enabler and her drug pusher. We terminated his services. Because she could not get her narcotic drugs, she began to drink beer instead and eventually stopped that because she was not feeling well. Mildred had other enablers, such as her live-in boyfriend. When we arrived in North Carolina because of her admittance to the hospital, Chauncey informed the boyfriend that he had to leave immediately. Mildred's boyfriend asked Chauncey to give him more time to get his things, and Chauncey said no, "It's time for you to leave." He gathered his belongings with the help of a friend and that terminated he and Mildred's dysfunctional relationship.

Mildred's chronic drinking was of great concern to Chauncey, Ecole, and I. We were concerned for her welfare based on the fact that she could fall and further injure herself, or that someone would take advantage of her instability. We suspected that someone had given her some type of drug and she suddenly began to experience hallucinations. Because Mildred sometimes associated with people who did not have her best interest at hand, we were fearful that someone would harm her by putting some hallucinating drug(s) in her drink. Our fears became a reality. Unfortunately, we were not present when the onset of hallucinations began. We suspected foul play because on a few occasions there were some shady characters that were in her presence

Seeing her in this state was baffling. It was extremely sad to witness our loved one talking to someone who was not present. It was all a figment of her imagination.

What Are Hallucinations?

According to The American Heritage College dictionary, Hallucinations are described as a false or mistaken idea; a delusion.

The National Institutes of Health defines Alcoholic Hallucinosis as a rare complication of chronic alcohol abuse characterized by predominantly auditory hallucinations that occur with, during, or after a period of heavy alcohol consumption. These hallucinations are typically auditory but may manifest as visual or tactile. Alcoholic hallucinations can occur 24 hours after the last drink and continues for about 24 hours. Symptoms consist of persecutory, auditory, or (most commonly) visual and tactile hallucinations; however, the patient's sensorium is otherwise clear. In the early stages, the patient recognizes frank hallucinations. Moreover, there are many causes of hallucinations, including: Being drunk or high, or coming down from such drugs like marijuana, LSD, cocaine (including crack), PCP amphetamines, heroin, ketamine, and alcohol. (Ketamine is used to put you to sleep for surgery and to prevent pain and discomfort during certain medical tests or procedures).

Mildred's hallucination was in full gear one particular winter night. She was standing in the frigid cold talking out of her head that someone had murdered her son, Chauncey. A neighbor overheard her talking and tried to get her to go back inside of her apartment. She was not successful and called the ambulance. There were no available rooms in neighboring psychiatric hospitals for this type of situation; therefore, she was transferred to a treatment facility in Tennessee, almost five hundred miles away. This was the beginning of her losing her independence and living on her own. She was unable to adequately care for herself. She had to be hospitalized for her illness.

After her return from the psychiatric hospital, she was transferred to Wake MED hospital in Raleigh, NC for further psychiatric evaluations. She was hospitalized for several weeks. The hospital contacted me at my residence in Maryland and informed me that she was being discharged, and I needed to get her. I gathered my things and headed to North Carolina.

It was apparent because of the hallucinations that she could no longer live alone. Chauncey, Ecole, and I needed to secure an assisted living facility as soon as possible. We visited several establishments that could accommodate her specific needs. After several visits, we located one that was perfect for her needs. The initial facility Mildred was admitted to did not have a good outcome. She was only a resident for a few days when she alleged that a resident spat in her food which led to her smacking an elderly woman in the face. The facility immediately discharged her and transported her back to Wake MED Hospital, where she had recently been discharged. Yet again, this was an unbelievable occurrence and we had to begin looking for another independent assistant living facility. Within a few days we located a facility that accepted her medical condition. She was accepted at Phoenix Assisted Care in Cary, North Carolina and was a resident at this facility for about two years.

Being a resident in the assisted living facility was reassuring because it seemed we could regulate her meds better. The doctors often rotated shifts. As a family, we asked them to discontinue some of her prescriptions. Sometimes they adhered to our requests and discontinued perhaps three of the prescriptions. It simply was not in her best interest to take these various prescriptions. On average, she was prescribed more than twenty narcotic and non-narcotic drugs to deal with her pain. She often complained of being in constant pain. She described severe pain in her legs and having body aches. Our immediate family suspected these were tactics she used because she wanted more prescription drugs. However, Mildred began to lose her appetite and remained irritable. On one occasion, Chauncey, Ecole, and I wanted her to leave the assisted living facility and visit with our family. But she refused to leave the facility. This was unusual behavior for her because any chance she had, she wanted to get out of there. There were times when I visited my family in North Carolina and often made arrangements for her to stay with us for long periods of time. To give her a new scenery and to keep her mind off her troubles, we'd stay at a beautiful hotel and relax. She especially enjoyed sitting poolside. Being away from the assisted living facility was a breath of fresh air for her. She really enjoyed those moments and so did I. There were other times when she would hang with us for the entire weekend. In those instances, we would grab lunch or dinner, catch a movie, and would visit family and friends. We all had a great time, and it was good to see her enjoy herself, even if it were just for a brief time frame. She deserved that to take her mind off her pain.

One evening she began to complain about excessive stomach pains and was transported to Wake Med Hospital. The hospital ordered a biopsy and decided against it and performed a magnetic resonance imaging (MRI) instead. It revealed that she had cancer and it had spread to other parts of her body.

(MRI is used in radiology to form pictures of the anatomy and the physiological processes of the body both in health and disease).

The doctors determined that in addition to the MRI, they needed to perform a computerized tomography (CT) scan.

(According to Healthline, CT scans can detect bone and joint problems, like complex bone fractures and tumors. If you have a condition like cancer, heart disease, emphysema, (Emphysema is a lung condition that causes shortness of breath) or liver masses, CT scans can spot it or help doctors see any changes. They show internal injuries and bleeding).

It showed the cancer had spread to her abdomen, right pelvic bone, and shoulders. There was fluid in her lungs, and they had collapsed, she had an enlarged heart, liver damage, enlarged lymphoid, and evidence of pelvic fractures. Also, the cancer had spread in her back vertebrae. After the doctors performed the MRI and CT scan, it was determined there would be no further treatment and she would be admitted to hospice. Ecole was the first person to receive this information since she lived in a neighboring city. She was so distraught that the social worker who delivered the news to her called the chaplain to comfort her and to talk with her about the situation. Ecole could not comprehend what they were saying because she was in total distress. Chauncey and I were telephoned about the situation and arranged to travel to North Carolina. He and I left the next day. The hospital physicians and social workers informed us there was nothing else they could do and referred us to Transitions Hospice Care in Raleigh, North Carolina. This level of hospice care is usually a short duration with a focus on pain and symptom management.

We were in shock and disbelief. We were overwhelmed with sadness and despair. What do we do now? How do we move forward? How do we carry out further instructions for admittance to hospice? How do we collect our thoughts with such sudden and tragic news? Hearing this news blindsided me. I was not expecting to hear that. I had to leave the room and went to the bathroom to cry. I could not keep it together this time. I bawled my eyeballs out. I will never forget the shock that appeared on Mildred's face when she was informed of her diagnosis. My sister was going to die! I grappled with the idea that she was going to be leaving me soon. This was all so sudden. I thought, "Is this really happening?" My time with her was slipping away! I needed more time to spend with her. More time to laugh. More time to go shopping with her. More time to visit with family and friends. More time to take her out to lunch and dinners. More time – I needed more time.

I had no control over the situation, and it was terribly difficult to see my sister dying. At some point in hospice, she was no longer talking. I frequently visited the nurses station inquiring about her pain medications. I wanted to do everything to make her feel better. She was starting to fade in her strength and was not allowed to eat food; she could only drink water. In her weakness, I gave her water and remembered my mother saying, "You never know who will give you your last drink of water." This meant to be kind to all people. You never know what the end will be. Many times, I had to leave out of her room because I felt sick to my stomach. I was overcome with pain and sorrow witnessing my sister in this state. The hardest part was that there was nothing I could do to make it better for her. My sister was dying!

As I sat by her bedside, so many thoughts ran through my mind. She would be leaving us soon. Mildred would stare into my eyes without saying a word. Her stare revealed to me that she was afraid of dying, at the same time, she was saying goodbye and declaring how much she loved me. When my daughter was alone in the room with her, she would ask, "Where is my sister?" I was her rock and she was well aware that I would be her foundation. I made her feel like she was never alone and that I would be right by her side to the very end. She knew I would not let her down. My goal was to make her last days as comfortable and as pleasant as possible.

As the reality of it all sank in deeper, we had to move swiftly. Since our family had less than two weeks before her death, we arranged her funeral simultaneously while visiting her in hospice. Ecole, Chauncey, and I made arrangements with cemetery officials. Collectively, we developed the funeral program by collecting and assembling photos, and we contacted some of our relatives who were pastors and requested their participation. We gathered all other details in planning her homegoing service. In order to carry out these tasks, I had to maintain my composure and be coherent. I remained focused on the matters at hand, but it was challenging to keep it together.

Chauncey received the awaited telephone call from hospice sometime after 12 midnight that his mother had passed. Mildred died on May 30, 2018. Chauncey, Ecole, and I were at my sister's apartment during our entire stay in North Carolina. Chauncey awakened Ecole and I and told us she had passed. We hugged each other and cried profusely. The anticipated death was upon us and I was filled with anguish. We gathered ourselves and got dressed to see her body and to say our goodbyes. It was one of the saddest days of my life. I didn't have the closure I needed because everything was moving too fast; I could barely think straight. I felt so lonely and asked the typical questions: Why? Why now? Why couldn't I have had more time? A flash flood of emotions overtook me as I reflected on the times we shared together. It felt like I lost a part of myself. The reality of her passing began to sink in for us; she was gone. It hurt so much because our immediate family was small and dwindling down. The primary adults now consisted of Chauncey, Ecole, and I.

For the next several days, we made notification telephone calls to family and friends, confirmed clergy and speakers for the funeral service, arranged for catering for the repast, and scheduled with the cemetery office for the final resting place. We had no choice but to quickly move forward because there was so much that needed to be done: Arrange for the retrieval of her body, meet with the official to arrange the cremation, and contact the funeral director.

Mildred spoke highly of her pastor and it was her request that he would eulogize her. I spoke with him about it and he honored her request. He also allowed the family to have the funeral at his church. When I met with him to work out the details, I had a tearful moment and cried from all the emotions that were pent up inside of me. Since there was so much to arrange, I did not have sufficient time to settle down and properly deal with my emotions. I was mentally exhausted from reviewing and signing documents. Through all the scurrying, I somehow managed to crack my front tooth and had to schedule a dental appointment. While at the dental office, the dentist informed me that he could not repair my front tooth. This was the tipping point that triggered the floodgates of tears. I cried so much that I actually frightened the dentist and his staff. I informed him that my sister died, and I could not walk around with a cracked tooth in the front of my mouth. I told him I was handling the funeral arrangements and could not be seen with a cracked tooth. The dentist was able to apply temporary braces that would hold until I returned home. Thank God he was compassionate and willing to come to my aid.

Mildred's death had me befuddled. When it was time to make the final payments for her burial, I could not remember my passwords to my credit cards. I couldn't even remember my home and cell phone numbers. My memory concerning numbers was temporarily gone. Chauncey actually had to put his cell phone in front of my face that revealed my home telephone number. Needless to say, the cemetery office could not process the payments. After several attempts to recall my passwords, the bank locked the access. Eventually, I went to the bank to change my passwords to further conduct business. Thank God Chauncey was nearby to help me during my temporary memory loss. He held it together well in accepting the passing of his mother.

I thought it was befitting to have him share his perspective and memories of his mother and the relationship they shared. I conducted an in-person interview with Chauncey. He related the following accounts concerning his mother's numerous hospitalizations, residency at assisted living facilities and when she was entering her final phase of life. He shared that when his mother died, he felt numbness and relief at the same time. He was relieved that his mother no longer had to struggle and suffer from the clutches of alcohol and prescription drugs. While she was in hospice, he knew what the outcome would be and what brought him solace was knowing that she would no longer be in pain. This helped him in remaining somewhat stable. These thoughts provided him the stability he needed to help funeralize his mother. When he reflected on the memories of his mother, he thought about her humor and how she always wanted to have a good time. He missed hearing her voice, seeing her, and the most affectionate expressions she would say to him, "Hey, son." He took pictures of her in the hospital, assisted living facility, hospice, and on her death bed. He said that in spite of her drinking, she was still a good person.

As Chauncey further discussed his relationship with his mother, he disclosed that there were dark sides to his mother. He gave an account of many embarrassing moments. The one incident that bothered him the most was when he was 15 years old. Chauncey had often invited his mother to his basketball games. She only attended one and it was a nightmare. This was a championship game and it was attended by a huge crowd of supporters. Mildred arrived at the basketball game intoxicated with some of her friends and decided to get on the court to catch the basketball. Some of his teammates were laughing. The coach took all the players off the court, talked with Chauncey for a while, and gave him some words of encouragement. Some of the teachers spoke with Mildred and eventually she and her friends left the school.

Chauncey also spoke of a time during elementary school of his mother's abhorrent behavior — showing up to his school drunk and

69

excessively loud. He could hear her before seeing her and would walk in the opposite direction to avoid her. Because of the verbal insults he received from his classmates about his mother he became a fearless fighter. No one would insult his mother in his presence because he would unleash his wrath and beat the crap out of someone. There was another time during junior high school when Mildred's behavior was just atrocious. She showed up intoxicated again and argued with him for no apparent reason. She defamed his character by spewing insults and then slapped him in his face. He avoided retaliating against her because he knew she was sick. When he was dating, he would go home first to make sure things were peaceful before taking his date to his home. These were very stressful times for him as a young man.

There was yet another incident outside my mother's residence on the sidewalk where Mildred had not been provoked and all of a sudden, she walked up to Chauncey, got in his face and arbitrarily began to fight him. She called him all kinds of names and I could not standby and allow her to continue. I intervened and stepped in the middle of them to confront her. She stepped off because she didn't want me to be upset with her. It was not often that I became angry but when I did my family was stunned and knew it had to be a bad situation. Because of Mildred's detestable behavior towards Chauncey, he would tell some of his friends that I was his mother. The story worked for a while and eventually it became apparent that I was not his mother. I loved and cared for him — still do — as if he were my son. Mildred was jealous of our relationship, but I could relate to Chauncey's dilemma. We needed stability because our mothers were chronic alcoholics. Chauncey eventually began to accept the fact that Mildred was his mother and that she was terribly sick. He came to an understanding that his mother had a disease that caused her to lash out in the way that she did. He eventually came to a place of forgiveness because he recognized she could not help herself.

Mildred and Chauncey's relationship became tolerable when he was about 30 years old. Whenever she was not drinking, which was seldom, they could have engaging conversations about sports and his two children, Chris and Maya. Chauncey regretted that his mother's behavior did not afford her the opportunity to be a better grandmother to his children. And she was too sick to bond with her great granddaughter, Chole. Chauncey wanted his mother to have a "normal" relationship with his children and granddaughter since she didn't have one with him. Mildred tried to do better with her grandchildren. She loved them dearly and there were times when it was apparent. She would often ask about them and wanted to visit with them. She saw them periodically and enjoyed her time with them. Her face lit up whenever she saw them. Their presence brought a smile to her face each time she saw them. It was good that they were able to spend these moments together. It was difficult each time the grandchildren visited with Mildred. Whether it was at the hospitals, assisted living facility, or hospice, they knew death would be the end result. They shed tears at her gravesite and were distraught that their grandmother was no longer with them.

One day Chauncey and five of his friends were hanging out and playing cards. One of the guys commented that he felt Chauncey and his closest friends lived an incredible life because they resided on Capitol Hill (known for middle-income housing). This guy lived in the projects. Chauncey allowed him to talk for a while about his life in the hood. After he finished telling his stories of his life of drugs and crimes, Chauncey began to share his story about his mother and cousins' addictions to drugs and alcohol. The guy stood up and gave Chauncey a hug. His other friend had no idea how bad things were for Chauncey. They perceived him in a certain way because of where he lived or how he presented himself. They had no idea of his struggles. This goes to prove that we should never make assumptions about people based on their appearances.

Chauncey's healing came from sharing with these gentlemen his story unabashedly. By doing so, it brought to light that their mothers were chronic alcoholics as well and they understood Chauncey's plight. This commonality was the bond they shared. He found others whom he could commiserate with. Today these men still meet up routinely to discuss their personal struggles and life in general. This support group has proven to be therapeutic for them. In dealing with the obstacles that life throws our way, it's good to have people in our lives to help us get through them. It's never easy doing it alone. Whether it's a close friend, a brother/sister, a counselor or pastor, it's best to have an outlet to express hidden feelings. Chauncey's story is one we can all learn from. We should all recognize the importance of having a support system in place. We cannot survive on our own. Indeed, we need each other.

In summary, there is a unique connection between sisters, even when the relationship may be strained. Even though Mildred and I were not close when we were younger, the sudden news of her impending death was a shock to my system. It was a bitter pill to swallow. During moments like these, we realize what's most important in life – family. Life and death situations will cause us to get our priorities in order. I could not walk around with any angst in my heart about anything my sister did to me and others. Drugs and alcohol controlled her life to the point where she could not get back to herself. They robbed her of her life.

Mildred died of cirrhosis of the liver and other complications. She was 67.

CHAPTER 7

Intervention

Alcohol and drug addictions tore through the fabric of my family. For years, I prayed, cried, and hoped my mother, husband, cousins, and sister would've been successful in recovering from these dependencies. When I discussed with them the option of going into treatment programs, they all expressed how important it was for them to get their lives together. I sometimes shared with them how their compulsive behaviors impacted me personally as well as other family members, hoping it would have made a difference in them changing their ways. I still made attempts to assist them. It was not uncommon for me to contact organizations and request brochures and other literature on substance abuse for them to seek help. I felt it was important for me to remain current on these matters as well. It was my belief that this information would assist me in helping them and myself. Unfortunately, they did not heed my warnings and suggestions and were not victorious in long-term treatment.

My mother was repeatedly in treatment only while she was hospitalized. She was seen by doctors that treated alcoholism and offered her solutions and referrals for treatment. Regrettably, my mother did not attend any programs on her own volition. There was a particular occasion where Mildred was disgusted with my mother's intoxication and called the authorities to admit her into detox. When I learned of this situation, I was appalled. How dare she initiate such an action. They both needed to be in a detox program. Mildred asserted herself and my mother was taken away for several days. There was no contact or visits, which made it quite difficult to deal with. The uncertainty of what was happening to my mother was another level of concern as it caused my anxiety to increase.

My husband participated in several alcohol and drug treatment programs. One particular program referred him to the Washington Psychiatric Institute (WPI). The WPI provides care to individuals coping with anxiety, mood disorders, chemical dependency, depression and other personality disorders. I met with the medical staff and it was apparent that I was suffering right along with him. His unpredictable behavior was likened to someone who was bipolar. Needless to say, he was not committed to the treatment offered by WPI or any other facility. Eventually his addictions got the best of him, causing him to succumb to his illness.

My sister and cousins made their share of attempts or had good intentions regarding their recovery. Mildred was a participant of in and outpatient care at hospitals and alcohol and drug treatment programs for many years. There were times when she remained sober for a week, but I don't ever recall her being sober for an entire month. Usually, when she was sober it was because she had been very sick and needed to recover. Henry participated in Alcoholics Anonymous treatment programs for many years. He made several attempts to stop drinking but he too was not successful. The only time he ceased drinking was when he became sick. Once he began to feel better, the drinking resumed. Henry's continuous drinking resulted in his hospitalization. As discussed in his chapter, he ended up in hospice where he eventually died. Rodney was a heroin addict. I know he drank alcohol from time to time but was uncertain of the severity. I am not aware if he ever went to a treatment facility. I did find a letter he mailed from jail to his mother where he stated he was going to stop using drugs – he, of course, was unsuccessful. Though each member tried to escape the clutches of this disease, it ultimately snuffed their lives out. Substance abuse not only impacted them but other family members as well. I

74

was like a cancer that spread through the core of my family. Everyone was affected in some capacity.

Caregivers

Today, I can say I am Finally, Free. I survived some of my past personal issues in caring for my loved ones who battled alcohol and drug abuse. Their addictions thrusted me into the role of caregiver for each of them. Taking on the responsibilities involved as their caregiver was a tremendous undertaking, to say the least. Making medical decisions, arranging memorial services and attending burials for so many family members brought on an enormous amount of stress to my system, but I had to make the hard decisions on behalf of each of them. It was difficult to witness my loved ones die as a result of substance abuse. Seeing them deteriorate right before my eyes was a lot to digest. I did not realize I had it in me to handle the pressure that accompanied being their caregiver. All I knew was that things had to be addressed and so I handled them since no one in my immediate family was prepared or willing to assume the responsibilities. I felt intense stress to provide adequate care for my family. Honestly, there were times when I was not sure how I was able to do it all. I was operating on pure adrenaline. I didn't give too much thought to myself. I just did what was required to get things done. In spite of it all, I pushed through for the sake of my family.

One of the downsides of being a caregiver is the tendency to neglect oneself. They are doers who are so focused on caring for others that in the process of doing so they overlook themselves. The responsibility of meeting and talking to health care officials about their family member's affairs and figuring out the best approach to resolve their health issues can be taxing on the mind and body. Pressures like these can cause caregivers to lose sleep, experience depression and suffer in silence because they may seem like the "strong ones" in the family and have to maintain this persona. Take it from me, as one who has gone through the experience, operating in this capacity can prove to be traumatic. It's not healthy at all.

"Emotional and psychological traumas are defined as the result of extraordinarily stressful events that devastate our sense of security, making one feel helpless in perilous times. **"**

I was the direct caregiver for Rodney and Henry and co-caregiver for Mildred. In being the caregivers for my sister Mildred, my daughter, nephew, and I collaborated and made sure she was well taken care of. We often sent her care packages based on what she requested of us. Since Ecole lived nearby, she would purchase the items and deliver them to her at the assisted living facility. I mailed her care packages, clothes, and money so she could get her nails and hair done. It was important to try and maintain a normal life as much as possible under the circumstances.

The Prevention of Blindness organization has a unique program to aid those in need of glasses at reduced rates or no cost at all.

According to Ophthalmologist, Payal Patell, MD, alcohol can cause several short-term effects on your eyesight. It can cause double vision, blurriness, and difficulty adjusting to brightness and light contract.

As I cared for Rodney, I was responsible for the dissemination of the money that was given to him by his late mother. He trusted me to handle his affairs and I maintained his finances. When he was released from prison, I brought him new clothes and other necessities that he needed to live comfortably. These purchases were done in moderation. After Rodney's death, I contacted the cemetery office to arrange for his burial since our family had previously purchased a plot. The wake service was held at a funeral home and his home going service was befitting to his character. It was a peaceful celebration of his life attended by immediate family and some of his close friends. As for Henry, while he was in hospice, it was especially challenging for me because at that particular time his mother and brother were deceased. Many times, my thoughts were to treat both of Aunt Beadie's sons as she would have. I treated them both with dignity and ensured they were comfortable while transitioning to leave this world.

In my opinion, caregiving is an important job; not to be taken lightly. It requires patience, love, and kindness. God made me a nurturer and I found this attribute to be an awesome benefit to the sick and oppressed. Prior to having to care for my family members, I never thought I could be a caregiver, but unbeknownst to me, God equipped me to do it. Sometimes we discover our strengths during our most difficult times. After coming through these times, I suggest that if someone finds themselves in this predicament, that they ask themselves a few questions: How do you want to be treated in your last days? Do you want someone to comfort and encourage you? Do you want someone to sit by your bedside and feed you when needed? What I've learned from being in this role is that we ought to be careful how we treat people. The reality is that roles change. We don't know when we will be on the receiving end, being in need of someone to care for us.

Furthermore, it is important that we find balance in taking care of our mental and physical health.

Since caregivers are known to neglect themselves in rescuing and caring for others, measures should be set in place to aid them in traversing this terrain. If you are not involved in a church and do not have a relationship with God, I encourage you to find a church where you can learn about God and build a relationship with Him. In my opinion, caregivers or victims of substance abuse cannot sustain themselves without God being in their lives. I can assert to this fact because I am alive and well. If it had not been for God on my side, I probably would not be here today; the stress alone could have taken me out. After years of traumatic events, you can only endure so much physically and emotionally. I strongly encourage you to contact and use the resources and organizations available to your family members, friends and victims of substance abuse.

What Is A Caregiver?

There are only four kinds of people in this world: (1) those who have been caregivers, (2) those who are currently caregivers, (3) those who will be caregivers and (4) those who will need caregivers. Caregiving is universal. - Rosalynn Carter, Former First Lady of the United States

According to Community Health at Johns Hopkins Bayview, in simple terms, a caregiver is a person who tends to the needs or concerns of a person with short or long-term limitations due to illness, injury or disability. The term "family caregiver" describes individuals who care for members of their family of origin, but also refers to those who care for their family of choice. This could be members of their congregation, neighbors or close friends. Family caregivers play a significant role in health care, as they are often the main source of valuable information about the patient.

Caregiving in the United States 2020 report from the American Association of Retired People (AARP) and the National Alliance for Caregiving (NAC) have a piercing message about the 53 million Americans who are currently family caregivers. The job is not only often tough, it's tougher than what researches found in their 2015 report. Family caregivers are in worst health than they were 5 years ago according to the AARP and NAC.

According to "Caregiving in the U.S. 2015," the national survey conducted by the NAC and the AARP Public Policy Institute, 40 million Americans are providing care for an adult family member or friend, yet few of these identify themselves as caregivers. Often, the things that define being a caregiver, such as helping a parent purchase and organize their medications or taking a friend to their doctor's appointments, just seems like simply doing what needs to be done when someone needs help.

Growing Numbers of Family Caregivers

Based on its survey of 1,392 caregivers (61%) women; average age; 49
providing 24 hours of care weekly), AARP and NAC say that roughly
21% of Americans are caregivers. And the number of those providing
caregiving for people 50 and older (41.8 million) has risen about 20%
since 2015.

Signs of Caregiving Stress
- Feeling overwhelmed or constantly worried.
- Feeling tired often.
- Getting too much sleep or not enough sleep.
- Gaining or losing weight.
- Becoming easily irritated or angry.
- Losing interest in activities you use to enjoy.
- Feeling sad.
- Having frequent headaches, body pain or other physical problems.

Legal Basics for Caregivers

1. **Power of Attorney (POA)**
    - § This allows your older adult to authorize someone to make legal decisions when they are no longer competent.
    - § POA also covers authority to make financial decisions.

2. **Durable Power of Attorney for Health care**
    (*also known as a health care proxy*)
    - § This allows your older adult to authorize someone to make all decisions regarding health care including healthcare providers, medical treatment, and end-of-life decisions.
    - § This power only goes into effect when older adults are unable to make decisions for themselves.

3. **Living Will or Advance Directive**
    - § This allows your older adult to state, in advance, what

kind of medical care they do and do not want to receive.

- § This also covers what life-support procedures they would not like to have.

- § This is used when a person isn't able to make their wishes known on their own.

4. Living Trust

- § This allows your older adult (the grantor) to create a trust and appoint someone (a trustee) to manage the assets when they aren't able to manage their finances.

- § A person or a financial institution can be the trustee.

5. Will

- § Your older adult will name an executor and beneficiaries.

- § The executor is the person who will manage your older adult's estate at the time of death.

- § Beneficiaries will receive the estate at the time of death.

What Happens if you Don't Plan Ahead

If no planning is done and your older adult becomes incapacitated, family members must ask a court to appoint a conservator or guardian.

A conservatorship can be difficult for families because almost every action or decision on behalf of your older adult must be court supervised and approved.

Are You a Caregiver?

A family caregiver can be someone caring for a spouse or parent, an extended family member, or even a friend or neighbor. Do you provide someone help with:

- Transportation to medical appointments?
- Purchasing or organizing medications?
- Monitoring their medical condition?
- Communicating with healthcare professionals?
- Advocating on their behalf with providers or agencies?
- Getting in and out of beds or chairs?
- Getting dressed?
- Bathing or showering?
- Grocery or other shopping?
- Housework?
- Preparing meals?
- Managing finances?

If you answered "yes" to any of the examples listed above, you are a caregiver and may benefit from the Called to Care program. This is a program offered by the Johns Hopkins Bayview Medical Center for family caregivers. It prepares and supports individuals caring for loved ones with health-related needs and limitations. If you reside outside of the Baltimore, MD area, seek out similar programs in your local jurisdiction.

Who, Caring For Who
The Typical African American Caregiver

African American caregivers are 47.7 years old on average. They are more often unmarried than all other racial and ethnic groups and report lower household incomes than non-Hispanic white and Asian caregivers. African American caregivers typically care for a parent, spouse, or grandparent who is 64.9 years old and has 1.7 conditions, usually a long-term physical condition. About half the time the recipient lives in the African American caregiver's home; more commonly than non-Hispanic whites.

Doing What, With What Other Help

African American caregivers have been caring for 5.2 years on average. They more often are in a high intensity care situation than either non-Hispanic white or Asian caregivers: providing 31.2 hours of care weekly. African American caregivers are typically the only unpaid caregiver helping their recipient and more provide care in isolation (no unpaid or paid help) than non-Hispanic whites.

Work and Finance

Most African American caregivers work while caregiving, for 37.5 hours per week on average and most reporting at least one impact on their work due to their caregiving role (typically going in late, leaving early, or taking off to provide care). African American caregivers report experiencing 2.4 financial impacts as a result of providing care — more than with non-Hispanic white or Asian caregivers — most commonly stopping saving, leaving bills unpaid or paying them late, or taking on more debt.

Health and Well-Being

About half of African American caregivers feel they had no choice in taking on the caregiving role, but the majority find a sense of purpose or meaning in that role – more so than non-Hispanic white or Asian caregivers. African American caregivers less often report being in excellent or very good health than non-Hispanic white caregivers.

****

RESOURCES

NAC
National Alliance for Caregiving
1730 Rhode Island Avenue, Suite 812
Washington, DC 20036

AARP
Family Caregiving
601 E Street, NW
Washington, DC 20049

Caregiving at the National Institutes of Health Clinical Center
10 Center Drive
Bethesda, MD 20892
Email: social_media@cc.nih.gov

U.S. Department of Veterans Affairs (VA)
VA Caregiver Support

As a family caregiver you play an important role in caring for the Veteran at home and in the community.

Caregiver Support Line, at 1-855-260-3274.

AARP has an online caregiving community where caregivers can join, for free, to talk with other caregivers and get answers from experts in the community. Facebook users can visit AARP Family Caregivers Discussion group to connect, share stories and get answers to caregiving questions at 1-877-333-5885, also available in Spanish at 1-888-971-2013.

Don't delay — get help today for yourself, family members, or friends.

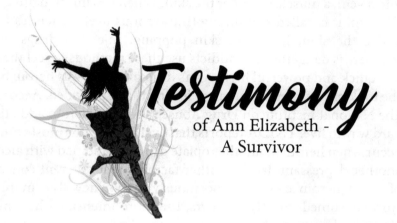

CHAPTER **9**

Testimony
of Ann Elizabeth - A Survivor

I conducted a telephone interview with my cousin, Ann Hilliard, where she recounted the following story: At the age of fourteen, Ann took her first sip of an alcoholic beverage. She along with six of her friends bought a gallon of Thunderbird. This wine was known for its striking yellow color and intoxicating effects. Initially it contained an alcohol content of about 20 percent, which was later lowered to 17.5 percent. Ann put her mouth on the gallon bottle of wine and took her first drink. After nearly consuming the entire bottle of wine, she fell out and hit her head. Because of her severe intoxication and being unaware of her surroundings, she was subsequently sexually molested by those whom she thought were her friends. The individuals who molested her were not her friends but were people she knew from around the way. She didn't really know them but for some reason she trusted them or felt safe being around them. She experienced blackouts as a result of drinking too much alcohol too quickly and was unable to manage what she was experiencing. After experiencing such an egregious act, she continued to increase her consumption of alcohol and drugs until she was 24 years old. This was a coping mechanism that she used to block out the horrendous experience she had with her friends.

Finally Free

At the age of 16, Ann began using several forms of narcotic drugs, (See Appendix A). She used a series of downers known on the street as "Black Beauties" heroin — which she snorted, skin popped and main lined. When injecting heroin, it's administered in certain ways: into a vein, a muscle or under the skin. When it is injected directly into the vein, it is called mainlining (intravenous use). When it's injected under the skin, it's called skin popping. Injecting drugs in these manners is dangerous but addicts use these methods to feel the effects of a quick and powerful high. Ann's drug of choice was heroin because she took pleasure in the lethargic feeling that it provided. According to The National Institute on Drug Abuse (TNIDA), heroin addiction is a hard way to live. TNIDA reports that overdose deaths most commonly occur when heroin or another opiate drug is combined with alcohol or another depressant drug. Another factor is that different concoctions of street heroin can vary enormously in potency. The more drugs Ann consumed, mostly downers, the more intensified her intake of alcoholic beverages became. Her alcoholic beverage of choice was bourbon whiskey. However, on an average day, she consumed 3 to 4 bottles of wine with each bottle content being 25 ounces of alcohol; which equals 3 cups per drink. During this particular time, a fifth of liquor cost $2.00.

Another incident occurred when Ann was a young adult. She was intoxicated and went with some male friends to listen to a band in Brandywine, Maryland. Again, she found herself in the same situation as a teenager where she was sexually molested by male friends and other men she did not know. This sexual abuse was the defining moment for her to begin the journey of recovery. Ann reported this gruesome rape that occurred to her mother. The following week while she was at work, her mother contacted her and provided her with the telephone number to the Washington Area Intergroup Association (WAIA). The WAIA is an anonymous, nonprofessional program of recovery based on fellowship among those who feel they have lost the ability to control their consumption of alcohol. WAIA is a nonprofit organization that makes referrals and provides literature on the Alcoholics Anonymous program. Ann contacted WAIA and attended an initial meeting. Afterwards, she was referred to Alcoholics Anonymous (AA). Ann states she was able to get to A.A. because she was God-inspired. Today, Ann remains a member of A.A. for identification purposes. She describes

86

identification purposes as relating to the formal introduction in A.A. meeting, (i.e., "Hello my name is Jane Doe and I am an alcoholic"). She continues to attend A.A. meetings because she does not want to drink alcohol or use drugs ever again. When asked what advice she has for people suffering from alcohol and drug abuse, Ann stated, "If a person is ready to stop drinking and using drugs they will. If not, they won't stop." According to a report in the Alcoholics Anonymous, 4th edition of The Doctor's Opinion, by William D. Silkworth, M.D. he states, "We believe, and so suggested a few years ago, that the action of alcohol on these chronic alcoholics is a manifestation of an allergy; that the phenomenon of craving is limited to this class and never occurs in the average temperate drinker. These allergic types can never safely use alcohol in any form at all; and once having formed the habit and found they cannot break it, once having lost their self-confidence, their reliance upon things human, their problems pile up on them and become astonishingly difficult to solve." Dr. Silkworth explains: "The sensation (produced by alcohol) is so elusive that while they admit to its injurious, they cannot after a time differentiate the true from the false. To them their alcoholic life seems the only normal one."

In conclusion, Ann has been a successful member of Alcoholics Anonymous, (A.A.) since July 19, 1973. She has been sober for 47 years! She has not had a drink or used drugs since, nor has she ever relapsed on any of the aforementioned substances. As a member of A.A., she has shared her story for 47 years with A.A. members and recovering alcoholics and drug abusers.

A compassionate person, Ann's willingness to help others trickled down into my personal life. The day she showed me her untiring support for Ecole and I was when my husband passed away. When I received the news that my husband had passed, I called Ann and asked her advice on how to tell my daughter. She suggested that I go into a quiet space, close the door, and talk to God. I took her suggestion and prayed fervently to God and He gave me the peace that I needed to talk to my daughter and go through the process. His death was overwhelmingly stressful, and Ann was a source of strength for me. She assisted me by contacting various entities to finalize funeral arrangements. At that particular time, my daughter was seven years old and had been diagnosed with petit mal seizures. This type of seizure causes its victims to lose awareness of their surroundings for a short time. For this reason, I was apprehensive about sharing the news with my daughter. I spent time in prayer and reached out to her neurologist to inform him of the matter and to seek advice on how to address the situation. The neurologist assured me that he would be available should Ecole's seizures become uncontrolled and required medical attention. The onset of her seizures would develop under stressful events and the frequency was sometimes every 3 to 5 minutes. However, the doctor and I did not know how she would respond to the loss of her father. I needed to gather my emotions before telling Ecole about his death. I waited a day to compose myself before giving her the news. Ecole went to school the next day after her father passed away. When she returned home from school, I sat her down and told her I had some bad news to disclose to her. Before I could tell her about her father, she asked, "Is something wrong with my daddy?" Obviously, my demeanor and facial expressions revealed I was about to deliver some bad news. I comforted her and we both cried and hugged each other. Overall, Ecole adjusted well to her father's death. She had such resolve and was able to move forward in a positive direction. After several months, we were able to find closure and share our fond memories of Michael. Thankfully for Ecole and I it all worked out favorably. We were able to grieve and move forward in life. There was no need to further contact the neurologist regarding this painful circumstance. Ecole survived this experience unscathed.

I am grateful for Ann's willingness and courage in sharing her story. She is a source of strength for so many, including myself. After twelve years of working as a Senior Systems Engineer at AVAYA, a Digital Communications Company, she is now enjoying her retirement. She is a devout Christian and serves in the "Prayer, Care, Praise, and Share Ministry" at her church. In this ministry, she is responsible for sending daily words of encouragement via email to the congregation. Ann is the only member of my immediate family who managed to successfully overcome alcohol abuse and drug addiction. I love and admire her for her devotion and dedication to helping recovering alcoholics and drug abusers. Her faithfulness and tenacity in maintaining her sobriety since 1973 are to be admired and acknowledged. She is a great example for others to follow. Ann currently resides in North Carolina.

Regrettably, I hate to report that several of my relatives who are alive today are alcoholics and drug abusers. They are absolutely aware of our family history of relatives passing away because of substance abuse. In lieu of this fact, it has not deterred them from using various substances, knowing that the inevitable outcome is death. The continuation of this family pattern is a generational curse. While I was surrounded by this stigma, I'm thankful to God that He was with me all along — preventing me from becoming a victim as well. He had greater plans for me and my future. I am forever grateful. I believe there are many individuals in denial about the harmful effects of substance abuse and its role on family members and friends. Long term addictions have a damaging effect on the brain. (see Appendix A) I encourage everyone to seek out resources to help in overcoming this disease.

10 CHAPTER

Scientific Research
Below are statistics on alcohol consumption

Alcohol is the most predominant substance of abuse among people in recovery treatment, as reported by a 2017 Recovery Brands survey. Out of all the survey responses, nearly 70% of people struggled with a drinking problem, and nearly 53% of people sought treatment for alcohol abuse more than any other substance. Regardless of how many abused substances exist, ethanol is the most pervasive.[3]

According to the National Survey on Drug Use and Health (NSDUH) 19.7 million American adults (aged 12 and older) battled a substance use disorder in 2017. [1]

Almost 74% of adults suffering from a substance use disorder in 2017, struggled with an alcohol use disorder. [1]

About 38% of adults in 2017 battled an illicit drug use disorder. [1] That same year, 1 out of every 8 adults struggled with both alcohol and drug use disorder simultaneously. [1]

Alcohol can kill you. Young people can and do die when they drink too much. Alcohol is the number one killer of young people. [6]

Alcohol causes more death and destruction than all the other illegal drugs combined. [6]

[6] Beyond the Influence, Understanding and Defeating Alcoholism, Katherine Ketcham and William F. Asbury with Mel Schulstad and Arthur P. Ciaramicoli, Ed.D., Ph.D.

An estimated 6.6 million children under the age of eighteen live in households with at least one alcoholic parent. [6]

According to a report issued by the National Institute on Alcohol Abuse and Alcoholism, in October 1998, approximately 10% to 35% of heavy drinkers develop alcoholic hepatitis and 10% to 20% develop cirrhosis of the liver. [4]

The report also names cirrhosis as being the 7th leading cause of death among young and middle-aged adults in American. It, further states that, "approximately 10,000 to 24,000 deaths from cirrhosis may be attributable to alcohol consumption each year." [4]

In 2017, 8.5 million American adults suffered from both mental health disorder and a substance use disorder, or co-occurring disorders. [1]

Drug abuse and addiction cost American society more than $740 billion annually in lost workplace productivity, health care expenses, and crime-related costs. [2]

Alcoholics Anonymous (A.A.) The primary purpose of A.A. is to stay sober and help other alcoholics to achieve sobriety. A.A. has more that 120,000 groups in more than 175 countries around the world, with more than 2 million members. [3]

According to the National Institute on Drug Abuse, drugs alter the way nerve cells normally send, receive, and process information. They do this by (1) initiating the brain's natural chemical messengers, (2) by over-stimulating the "reward circuit" of the brain (3) flooding the brain with excess chemicals and (4) binding to receptors in the brain. [2]

Alcoholism – an Illness "Al-Anon Faces Alcoholism" by Joan K. Jackson, Ph.D.

Today we are willing to accept the idea that, as far as we are concerned, alcoholism is an illness, a progressive illness which can never be "cured," but which like some other illnesses, can be arrested. [3] We understand now that once a person has crossed the invisible borderline from heavy drinking to compulsive alcoholic drinking, that person will always remain an alcoholic. So far as we know, there can never be any turning back to "normal" social drinking. "Once an alcoholic, always an alcoholic" is a simple fact we have to live with. [3]

We have also learned that there are a few alternatives for alcoholics. If they continue to drink, their problem will become progressively worse; they seem assuredly on the path to skid row, to hospitals, to jails or other institutions, or to early graves. The only alternative is to stop drinking completely, to abstain from even the smallest quantity of alcohol in any form. If they are willing to follow this course, and to take advantage of the help available to them, a whole new life can open up for alcoholics. [3]

"It is no longer possible to consider alcoholism as a disease affecting only the alcoholic…The relationship between the alcoholic and the family is not a one-way relationship…"It is now believed that the most successful treatment of alcoholism involves helping the alcoholic and those members of the family who are directly involved in the alcoholic's behavior."
"Al-Anon Faces Alcoholism" by Joan K. Jackson, Ph.D.

Spoken by someone who wrestled with alcoholism:

"If drinking is interfering with your work, you're probably a heavy drinker. If your work is interfering with your drinking, you're probably an alcoholic." - *Anonymous*

"I always wanted to have a life. In treatment, I discovered that drug use had cost me my life." - *Anonymous*

Is Alcohol Use Disorder a Disease?
Periodically, controversy flares over whether alcohol use disorder is a disease. Disease may be defined broadly, but in the strict medical sense

it refers to a clearly identified physical process that is pathological. A critical feature of the definition is that once a disease is contracted, the afflicted individual has no control, or is not responsible, for the disease running its course. Typically, when alcohol use disorder is called a disease, the traditional medical model of disease is the referent. [5]

How is Alcoholism Classified?

According to Alcoholics Anonymous (A.A.), alcoholism is classified as a disease. As explained in the book Alcoholics Anonymous, Kurt N.* (In keeping with A.A.'s tradition of anonymity, author's name has been omitted). "Those who do not recover are people who cannot or will not completely give themselves this simple program, usually men and women are constitutionally incapable of being honest with themselves…There are those, too, who suffer from grave emotional and mental disorders, but many of them (not all) do recover if they have the capacity to be honest."

Brief Interventions for Alcohol Problems:

Brief interventions can be as simple as feedback about the consequences of heavy alcohol use for a person (for example, "You have some liver problems, and we traced it to your drinking") or advice to cut down or stop drinking. They are based on the idea that alcohol problems exist on a continuum of severity and that interventions can occur at any point along the continuum. The research has shown that, for the most part, brief interventions have been used with people who have mild to moderate alcohol problems; they are effective compared to no treatment in reducing alcohol consumption to below "risk" levels. There is some speculation about who is most helpful by brief interventions and why they work. These clearly are topics for future research. [5]

Alcohol and the Liver

The most serious and life-threatening of alcohol's liver assaults is cirrhosis. Alcohol dependence is the leading cause of cirrhosis, which is the eighth leading cause of death by disease in the United States and kills about 25,000 people a year (National Institute of Health, 2000; Stinson, Grant, & Dufour, 2001). Drinking must be prodigious and long-term for someone to develop alcohol-related cirrhosis. (Drug Use & Abuse, Seventh Edition). For those who do get cirrhosis, the condition is not reversible, and only half are still alive five years after receiving the initial diagnosis. Cirrhosis is a chronic inflammatory disease of the liver involving cell death and the formation of scar tissue. Alcohol hepatitis may or may not precede it. Death results from cirrhosis because the liver fails to metabolize various toxins, such as ammonia, and those toxins accumulate in the body.

Research Related to Alcoholics Anonymous Effectiveness:

The question of how effective A.A. is can be difficult to answer. One reason for the difficulty is the A.A. emphasis on the anonymity of its members. The principle of anonymity is a major part of the "Twelve Traditions of A.A., which are a set of principles or guidelines adopted in 1950 for the operation of A.A.

> (a) it is not possible to predict who will affiliate with A.A., except that it seems that people who have severe alcohol problems are more likely to join; (b) among people who do join A.A., it is not clear who will do well and who will not; (c) people who go to A.A. before, during, or after receiving other forms of treatment do as well as if not better than people who do not volunteer to go to A.A.; (d) A.A. participation is associated with relatively high abstinence rates but with average overall improvement in drinking rates; people who achieve abstinence seem to participate in A.A. more than those who moderate their drinking or who continue to drink at a problem level. (Emrick, 1989).

People's success in A.A. may be related to processes such as ways to cope with stress, beliefs that one can cope effectively in different situations without alcohol, and commitment to abstinence from alcohol (Morgenstern et al., 1977).

UNDERSTANDING ALCOHOLISM
The world's most misunderstood disease!

Unfortunately, like many other diseases, medical experts tell us that untreated alcoholism is nearly 100% fatal and will almost inevitably result in the premature death of the alcoholic. The American Medical Association now recognizes alcoholism as a disease. Many scientific studies have shown that genetics, not character or will power, is the key factor in determining whether or not one will become an alcoholic. [6]

According to Alcoholics Anonymous, alcoholism is a cunning and baffling disease, and it is not unusual for it to skip one or more generations. So even if neither of your parents were alcoholics –— or even "heavy drinkers" — you could still carry the alcoholism gene or genes. [6]

Ask yourself: Is there any evidence of alcoholism anywhere in my family of origin? If so, even though you don't like the idea, you could be (or be pre-programmed to become) an alcoholic. [6]

WHAT DO YOU THINK?

1. The highest rates of heavy drinking, and thus the greatest vulnerability to drinking problems, are in men between the ages of 40 and 45.

   False - The highest rates are in younger men, ages 18 to 25.

2. It is difficult to consume a lethal dose of alcohol.

   False - It is all too easy. The lethal dose 50 (LD50) of alcohol in humans is about equal to drinking a fifth (25.3oz) of whiskey in an hour. This is not too hard to do, and it has been done with dire consequences during events such as fraternity hazing.

3. If you drink a lot and black out, it means you have lost consciousness.

   False - Blackouts are the loss of memory for events that occur while under the influence of a drug (in this case, alcohol). A drinker who experiences a blackout is fully conscious when nonrecalled events happen. 5

4. Alcohol causes violent behavior.

   False - Alcohol is correlated with the occurrence of violent behavior, but cognitive, social, and environmental factors must also be used to explain the alcohol-violence association.

5. The cognitive deficits that seem to occur in some people as a result of years of heavy drinking are reversible.

   True - At least when there is not severe structural damage to the brain, as in Korsakoff's syndrome, many of the cognitive deficits that may occur are reversible with prolonged abstinence from alcohol.

6. The majority of individuals with severe alcohol use disorder eventually develop cirrhosis of the liver.

False - Some, but only a majority of about 10% to 20% of chronic heavy drinkers, certainly do develop cirrhosis. 5

WHAT DETERMINES IF A PERSON IS AN ALCOHOLIC?

Although there are numerous "tests" one can take to determine if he or she is an alcoholic, alcoholics generally find that once they start drinking, they have little or no control over the amount they drink. According to Dr. William D. Silkworth, the phenomenon of craving is an irresistible physical sensation that occurs once an alcoholic has taken that first or second drink ... a sensation "that never occurs in the average temperate drinker." Obviously then, the body of an alcoholic reacts differently to alcohol than the bodies of non-alcoholics.

TEST ONE
Suggested by the National Institute on Alcohol Abuse and Alcoholism

One "yes" answer suggests a possible alcohol problem. More than one "yes" answer means it is highly likely that a problem exists.

Q.   Have you ever felt you should cut down on your drinking?

Q.   Have people annoyed you by criticizing your drinking?

Q.   Have you ever felt bad or guilty about your drinking?

Q.   Have you ever had a drink first thing in the morning to steady your nerves or to get rid of a hangover?

TEST TWO

A popular test developed years ago in the Chicago area, based on information found in "12 Steps and 12 Traditions," of the Alcoholics Anonymous program. It was created to determine whether or not you have passed the point of "no return," and to see if you are still able to control your drinking. The procedure is to drink just two ounces of alcohol each evening, and then not touch a drop until the next, at which time you will drink only two ounces again. Try to keep this up for at least a week.

If you are unable to control your drinking in this manner, you are probably an alcoholic.

TEST THREE

Developed by Substance Abuse and Mental Health Services Administration National Clearing House for Alcohol and Drug Information

Q. Do you ever experience "the sensation of craving" — a strong, irresistible compulsion to have another drink?

Q. Have you ever lost the ability to control your drinking, drinking far more than you intended to?

Q. Have you ever experienced withdrawal symptoms, such as nausea, sweating, shakiness, and anxiety when the use of alcohol was stopped after a period of heavy drinking?

Q. Do you find that you need to keep drinking greater amounts of alcohol in order to "get high?"

If you answered "yes" to any of these questions, chances are good that you may well have a problem with alcohol.

CAN ALCOHOLISM BE CURED?

Unfortunately, as far as can be determined, science has not yet been able to come up with a way to turn an alcoholic into a normal drinker. It seems that once a person has experienced the so called "phenomenon of craving," it becomes impossible for him or her to ever drink normally again. The only solution appears to be complete abstinence.

By this time, however, most alcoholics have become so psychologically addicted to alcohol that they find it almost impossible to leave it alone without outside help.

CAN ALCOHOLISM BE TREATED?

Yes, fortunately the disease of alcoholism can usually be arrested if the alcoholic truly has a desire to stop drinking. Perhaps the best-known treatment program for alcoholics is Alcoholics Anonymous, which to date has helped millions of alcoholics learn how to live sober, happy, and productive lives.

IS ALCOHOLISM HEREDITARY?

It has been determined that almost invariably alcoholics come from families that had problems with alcohol. Researchers who have studied this field have also found that there is substantial evidence that shows that one's potential of becoming an alcoholic is indeed genetic. In fact, a report recently released by the National Institute on Alcohol Abuse and Alcoholism classifies alcoholism as a complex, multi-genetic disease "influenced by many genes located in different areas of a person's DNA."

Further intensifying the genetic predisposition to alcoholism is the fact that children from alcoholic homes almost invariably marry one another. Almost without exception, every married alcoholic determined by Kurt N.* is married to another alcoholic, or, if not to an alcoholic, to someone with alcoholism somewhere in his or her family origin.

*The author's name has been omitted in keeping with the Alcoholics Anonymous tradition of anonymity.

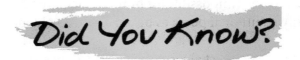

PHYSIOLOGICAL EFFECTS

Alcohol impairs memory. Its acute effects are on short-term memory, and when high Blood Alcohol Concentrations (BAC) are reached rapidly, a blackout may occur. Blackouts are an individual's amnesia about events when drinking, even though there was no loss of consciousness. For example, a person who had a lot to drink the night before may wake up and have absolutely no recollection of where he or she parked the car. Blackouts are thought to result from a failure in the transfer of information in short-term memory to long-term memory. [5]

EFFECTS OF CHRONIC HEAVY DRINKING

Chronic heavy use of alcohol may have numerous physiological and psychological effects. All the effects involve increased dysfunction, and some may be fatal. Some chronic alcohol effects are caused directly by alcohol's toxicity to the body, such as damage to the liver. Other effects are indirectly related to long-term heavy drinking. [5]

Changes That May Point to Substance Abuse:
A Checklist for Families

PHYSICAL HEALTH OR APPEARANCE
- Poor grooming or disheveled clothing
- Unwanted weight loss or gain
- Pale, cool skin
- Facial flushing
- Puffiness or bloating
- Wearing dark glasses at inappropriate times
- Tremors
- Drowsiness at inappropriate times of day

MOOD OR EMOTIONAL BEHAVIOR
- Irritability
- Mood swings
- Unjustified outbursts of anger
- Tearfulness or sadness
- Expressions of hopelessness
- Giddiness or irrational laughter
- Social isolation

PSYCHOLOGICAL CHANGES
- Confusion
- Unexplained memory loss
- Paranoia
- Delusional thinking
- Hallucinations

OCCUPATIONAL OR EDUCATIONAL STATUS
- Poor performance at work
- Job termination
- Decline in grades at school
- Neglect of favorite school activities
- Absenteeism at work or school

What are treatments for drug addiction?

According to Substance Abuse and Mental Health Services Administration, there are many options that have been successful in treating drug addiction, including:

- Behavior counseling

- Medication

- Medical devices and applications used to treat withdrawal symptoms or deliver skills training.

- Evaluation and treatment for co-occurring mental health issues such as depression and anxiety.

- Long-term follow-up to prevent relapse.

A range of care with a tailored treatment program and follow-up options can be crucial to success. Treatment should include both medical and mental health services as needed. Follow-up care may include community or family-based recovery support systems.

Ways to Help a Friend Struggling with Drug Addiction

1. Educate yourself about signs of addiction
2. Have a conversation and encourage treatment
3. Offer love and support
4. Group intervention may be the way to go

RESOURCES

Alcoholics Anonymous General Service Office
P.O. Box 459, Grand Central Station
New York, NY 10163
Tel. (212) 870-3400
www.aa.org

Alcoholics Victorious
Tel. (816) 561-0567
www.alcoholicsvictorious.org

Alcoholics for Christ
1316 N. Campbell Road
Royal Oak, MI 48067
www.alcoholicsforchrist.com

Al-Anon Family Group Headquarters
1600 Corporate Landing Parkway
Virginia Beach, VA 23454-5617
Tel. (888) 425-2666
www.al-anon.alateen.org

Association of Intervention Specialists
313 W. Liberty Street, Suite 129
Lancaster, PA 17603
Tel. (717) 392-8488
www.associatinofinterventionspecialists.org

Celebrate Recovery
Tel. (800) 723-3532
www.celebraterecovery.com

Join Together
A national clearinghouse for information regarding recent tests and development in the field of alcoholism treatment.
www.jointogether.org

National Institute on Alcohol Abuse and Alcoholism
5635 Fishers Lane, MSC 9304
Bethesda, MD 20892-9304
www.niaaa.nih.gov

SAMHSHs' National Clearing House for Alcohol
and Drug Information
P.O. Box 2345
Rockville, MD 20847-2345

The National Council on Alcoholism and Drug Addiction
244 East 58th Street, 4th Floor
New York, NY 10022
Tel. (212) 269-7797
www.ncadd.org

National Helpline – Substance Abuse and Mental Health Services Administration (SAMHSA)

1-800-662-4357. This is a free, confidential, 24/7, 365 days a year treatment referral and information services (in English and Spanish) for individuals and families facing mental and/or substance use disorders. This service provides referrals to local treatment facilities, support groups, and community-based organizations. Callers can also order free publications and other information.

Find alcohol, drug, or mental health treatment facilities and programs around the country at www.findtreatment.samhsa.gov.

Find information on locating practitioners and treatment program authorized to treat opioids such as heroin or prescription pain reliever at:
www.samhsa.gov/medication-assisted-treatment/practitioner program-data/treatment-practitioner-locator.

Finally Free

Find treatment programs in your state that treat addiction and dependence on opioids, such as heroin or prescription pain relievers, at www.Dpt2.samhsa.gov/treatment/.

Hazelden Betty Ford Foundation
Resources for Families Facing Alcohol and other Drug Addictions
1-888-754-1376

The Hazelden Betty Ford Foundation is a force of healing and hope for individuals, families and communities affected by addiction to alcohol and other drugs. It is the nation's leading nonprofit provider of comprehensive inpatient and outpatient treatment for adults and youth.

Drug Treatment, Alcohol and Substance Abuse Programs
If you or a loved one meet the criteria for alcohol abuse or dependence and are ready to seek help, call the toll-free number.
1-877-475-1664
www.DrugAbuse.com.

An American Addiction Centers Resource
Get the Facts on Alcohol Abuse
The most readily available socially acceptable form of abuse comes from alcohol. It can also be one of the most destructive and hardest to leave behind.

ACKNOWLEDGEMENTS

First and foremost, I am grateful to God for His presence in my life. As a member of The Shepherd's House International Christian Church (TSHICC), I would like to acknowledge my Senior Pastor, R. Kevin Matthews, for his leadership, love, and wisdom. I'd also like to extend a special thank you to First Lady Malissa Matthews for being a source of inspiration and encouragement to the body of Christ. I am blessed to be a member of a church that stresses the importance of biblical teachings and making disciples. Pastor Kevin — thank you for offering the MasterLife Program to us (church body). As a result of participating in this class, I was exposed to divine Christian women who enriched my life. These teachers, facilitators, and group members were amazingly encouraging, inspiring and loving during this process. To the following ladies, I'd like to say thank you for making this season in my life one of personal growth and one that I enjoyed: Minister Victoria Marie Stewart, Linda R. Thompson, Marie Whitmyer, Mojisola Agbedi, Beverly Bradley, Iris Butler, Beverly Castleberry, and my prayer partner, Linda Drew. Being a member of this group allowed healing and learning to manifest in a non-judgmental manner. Ladies, you were all awe-inspiring and I'm so glad I met each of you.

Thriving on teaching biblical principles, TSHICC also offers classes that enhance the lives of its members. Again, thank you, Pastor Kevin for having the foresight in offering the How to Finish Strong seminar. Stemming from the book, See You At The Finish Line: Cultivating The Mindset Of A Finisher by Dr. Pamela Love Manning, this seminar was the catalyst that caused me to take a leap of faith and finally write my own book. By attending, I was able to work with a leadership coach who was instrumental in my staying the course and completing my book. Sherri Cox, thank you for being in my corner, cheering me on and encouraging me while I was writing this book. I appreciate you for everything you've done for me in crossing the finish line and finishing strong.

Again, special thanks to my family: To my daughter, Ecole — thank you for your support through it all; Chauncey (nephew), thank you for contributing to this book by sharing your personal experiences with your mom. I appreciate your honesty and transparency; Ann Hilliard (my dear cousin), thank you for your contribution to this book. Sharing your compelling testimony of overcoming substance abuse, I know will impact the lives of others. A special thank you to Beverly Castleberry for your willingness to provide constructive feedback when asked. I appreciate you. Lastly, I would like to thank my editor, Andrea L. Reid, for working closely with me on this book project. Thank you for your suggestions, advice, and coaching along the way. I am proud of the final outcome and the effort that you put forth to ensure my story was told correctly.

ABOUT THE AUTHOR

Edith Butler is a native Washingtonian who loves God and is devoted to her spiritual destiny. She believes we should all work towards our destiny; doing what God has created us to do. She is a dynamic speaker and advocate for women in business with over twenty-five years of experience. She promotes and develops businesses on technical assistance, business operations and federal procurement and contracting. Edith is the owner of EGB Consulting, LLC, a small business enterprise that offers business development services such as portfolio development, and research and development. The company's vision is to help entrepreneurs succeed by providing opportunities that will enhance their businesses.

From her experience with the loss of family members to substance abuse, she has developed an innate ability to assist and care for others. She formerly served as a Stephen Minister where she offered quality care to women experiencing difficult times and those dealing with grief. Stephen Ministers are lay congregation members trained by their congregation's Stephen Leader to provide one-on-one care to those experiencing difficult times in life such as grief, divorce, job loss chronic or terminal illness, and relocation.

Edith has a Bachelor of Arts degree in Psychology. She acquired her Level III Federal Acquisition Certification for Contracting from the Federal Acquisition Institute. She retired from the United States government as a procurement analyst. Currently, she is a member, writer, and editor of the Ladies Lit Book Club. In her spare time, she enjoys reading different genres of books, writing poetry, and listening to jazz and gospel music. She is also the proud mother of daughter, Ecole Butler. She is blessed to be grandmother to Michael Butler. Her daughter and grandson reside in North Carolina. Edith lives in Maryland where she is enjoying her retirement.

For virtual speaking engagements, please contact:
Edith G. Butler
3540 Crain Hwy. #263
Bowie, MD 20716
(301) 706-7243
Email: ebbooksfinally@gmail.com
Website: ebbooksfinally.com

Edith is a determined and brilliant woman of God who has successfully surpassed problems of emotional trauma which began in childhood through young adulthood. As a friend and confidante, she unveiled painful events in her life that transpired many years ago. As a former colleague, I am thrilled about the courage Edith exemplified in sharing her story and how she overcame the traumas brought on by various family members who were addicted to drugs and alcohol.

- Richard L. Kirby

Edith Butler describes a moving, captivating, and personal story of alcoholism and drug abuse within her family. The compelling display of God's deep and abiding love permeates from her spirit in every attempt to keep loved ones from falling further into the depths of addiction. She admits to bouts of shame, anxiety, and embarrassment, but her steadfast commitment to love of family is a master class life lesson. Edith embraces with remarkable honesty and tenacity her story with all the plots, twists and turns. However, out of it is a profound and powerful message of hope, peace, and above all else, the love of God.

-Beverly Castleberry, Certified Health Coach and Personal Trainer

In Finally, Free, Edith is transparent in sharing her story of having family members who were addicted to drugs and alcohol and the impact it had on her and other family members. As a private person, this was not an easy feat. However, she courageously shows us how to press through times of longsuffering while completing the assignment that we are called to do. Finally, Free not only shares moving stories but serves as a resource to assist anyone in need of counseling or treatment for addictions. This book is a great read where others can glean from the stories shared within these pages.

- Sherri L. Cox, Founder of iCan Global Ministries

APPENDIX A
Glossary of Terms

Addiction – In reference to drugs, overwhelming involvement with using a drug, getting an adequate supply of it, and having a strong tendency to resume use of it after stopping for a period.

Addictive personality – The hypothesis of a personality structure common to all people with substance use disorders.

Blackout – Failure to recall events that occurred while drinking even though there is no loss of consciousness.

Cocaine - is a colorless or white crystalline alkaloid extracted from coca leaves, sometimes used in medicine as a local anesthetic and widely used as an illicit drug. 2

Crack Cocaine - is purified cocaine in pellet form that is smoked through a pipe and is highly addictive, its preparation by breaking cocaine crystals into pellets. 2

Disulfiram – A drug that interferes with the metabolism of alcohol so that people soon feel very ill if they drink while on a regimen of disulfiram. The drug may be used as part of a treatment program for alcohol dependence. 5

Downer – A depressant or sedative drug.

Drug – Broadly defined as any chemical entity or mixture of entities not required for the maintenance of health but that alters biological function or structure when administered.

Drug Abuse – Any use of drugs that caused physical, psychological, legal, or social harm to the individual use or to others affected by the drug user's behavior.

Ethanol - An intoxicating ingredient of many alcoholic beverages such as beer, wine and distilled spirits.

Heroin – An odorless, bitter crystalline compound, that is derived from morphine and is a highly addictive narcotic. Heroin is more potent than morphine and has become the major opiate drug of abuse. (Drug Use & Abuse, Seventh Edition)

Intoxication - A transient state of physical and psychological disruption caused by the presence of a toxic substance, such as alcohol in the central nervous system.

Morphine – A derivative of opium best known as a potent pain-relieving medication.

Narcotic- A central nervous system depressant that contains sedative and pain-relieving compounds.

Opiate – 1. Any of various sedative narcotics containing opium or one more of its derivates. 2. A drug or other substance effects similar to those containing opium or its derivatives. 3. Something that dulls the senses and induces relaxation or torpor.

Oxycodone – A narcotic alkaloid, related to codeine and used as an analgesic and a sedative chiefly in the form of its hydrochloride salt.

Synthetic Marijuana – A psychoactive "designer drug" that is synthesized from various amphetamine like chemicals and can be inhaled, swallowed, smoked and injected.

REFERENCES

Alcoholic 1. Related to or resulting from alcohol. 2. Containing or preserved in alcohol. 3. Suffering from alcoholism. A person suffers from alcoholism. 2

What is Alcoholics Anonymous?
Alcoholics Anonymous, A.A. is a worldwide fellowship of men and women who help each other to stay sober. They offer the same help to anyone who has a drinking problem and wants to do somethings about it. Since they are alcoholics themselves, they have a special understanding of each other. They know what the illness feels like — and they have learned how to receive from it in A. A. Both the American Medical Association and the British Medical Association, chief organization of doctors in those countries, also have said that alcoholism is an illness.

What is Alcoholism?
As Alcoholics Anonymous, A.A. sees it, alcoholism is an illness. Alcoholics cannot control their drinking, because they are ill in their bodies and in their minds (or emotions), A.A. believes if they do not stop drinking, their alcoholism almost always gets worse and worse. In a report recently released, the National Institute on Alcohol Abuse and Alcoholism classifies alcoholism as a complex, multi-genetic disease "influenced by many genes located in different areas of a person's DNA."

Health Risks of Alcoholism
The U.S. Center for Disease Control and Prevention (CDC) reports that not only does alcohol kills an estimated 75,000 American each

year, but that it cuts their lives short by an average of 30 years (CC Weekly Report, September 24, 2004, "Alcohol Attributable Deaths").

What are the symptoms?
Not all alcoholics have the same symptoms, but many — at different stages in the illness — show these signs. They find that only alcohol can make them feel self-confident and at ease with other people; often want "just one more" at the end of a party; look forward to drinking occasions and thinks about them a lot; get drunk when they had not planned to; try to control their drinking by changing types of liquor, going on the wagon, or taking pledges, sneak drinks; lie about their drinking; hide bottles; drink at work (or school); drink alone; have blackouts (that is, cannot remember the next day what they said or did the night before); drink in the morning, to relieve severe hangovers, guilty feelings and fears, fail to eat and become malnourished; get cirrhosis of the liver; shake violently, hallucinate, or have convulsions when withdrawn from liquor.

What can the families of alcoholics do?
A.A. is just for the alcoholics, but two other fellowships can help their relatives. One is Al-Anon Family Groups. The other is Alateen for teenagers who have alcoholic parents.

Cirrhosis of the Liver
Cirrhosis of the liver is a chronic disease of the liver marked by degeneration of cells, inflammation, and fibrous thickening of tissue. It is typically a result of alcoholism or hepatitis.

Cirrhosis
1. A chronic disease of the liver marked by replacement of normal tissue with fibrous tissue, resulting from alcohol abuse, nutritional deprivation, or infection. 2. Chronic interstitial inflammation of any tissue or organ. [2]

Trauma
Trauma is often the result of an overwhelming amount of stress that exceeds one's ability to cope, or integrate the emotions involved with that experience. Trauma may result from a single distressing

experience or recurring events being overwhelmed that can be precipitated in weeks, years, or even decades as the person struggles to cope with the immediate circumstances, eventually leading to serious, long-term negative consequences. [2]

Because trauma differs between individuals, according to their subjective experiences, people will react to similar traumatic events differently. In other words, not all people who experience a potentially traumatic event will actually become psychologically traumatized.

However, it is possible for some people to develop post-traumatic stress disorder after being exposed to a major traumatic event. This discrepancy in risk rate can be attributed to protective factors some individuals may have that enable them to cope with trauma; they are related to temperamental and environmental factors from among others. Some examples are resilience characteristics, and active seeking help. [2]

Protective Factors are conditions or attributes (skills, strengths, resources, supports or copying strategies) in individuals, families, communities or the larger society that help people deal more effectively with stressful events and mitigate or eliminate risk in families and communities. [2]

People take drugs for many reasons: peer pressure, relief of stress, increased energy, to relax, to relieve pain, to escape reality, to feel more self-esteem, and for recreation. The United States has the highest substance abuse rate of any industrialized nation. Government statistics (1997) show that 36% of the United States population has tried marijuana, cocaine, or other illicit drugs. [3]

Alcoholic Anonymous is an international fellowship of men and women who have had a drinking problem. It is a nonprofessional, self-supporting, multiracial, apolitical, and available almost everywhere. There are no age or education requirements. Membership is open to anyone who wants to do something about his or her drinking.

As explained in the book, Alcoholics Anonymous: "Those who do not recover are people who cannot or will not completely give themselves this simple program, usually men and women are constitutionally incapable of being honest with themselves...There are those, too, who suffer from grave emotional and mental disorders, but many of them (not all) do recover if they have the capacity to be honest."
Understanding Alcoholism, by Kurt N.*
*In keeping with A.A's tradition of anonymity, Author's name has been omitted.
Drug Use & Abuse, Seventh Edition by Stephen A. Maisto, Mark Galizio, and Gerald J. Connors.

Citations:

1 An American Addiction Centers Resource
2 National Institute on Drug Abuse. (2017). Trends & Statistics.
3 Alcoholics Anonymous. (2018). Estimated Worldwide A.A. Individual and Group Membership and Alcoholics Anonymous (2017) The is A.A. An Introduction to the A.A. Recovery Program
4 National Institute on Alcohol Abuse and Alcoholism
5 Drug Use & Abuse, Seventh Edition, Stephen A. Maisto, Mark Galizio, Gerald J. Connors
6 Beyond the Influence, Understanding and Defeating Alcoholism, Katherine Ketcham and William F. Asbury wth Mel Schulstad and Arthur P. Ciaramicoli, Ed.D., Ph.D.

CPSIA information can be obtained
at www.ICGtesting.com
Printed in the USA
BVHW050049080421
604338BV00008BA/740